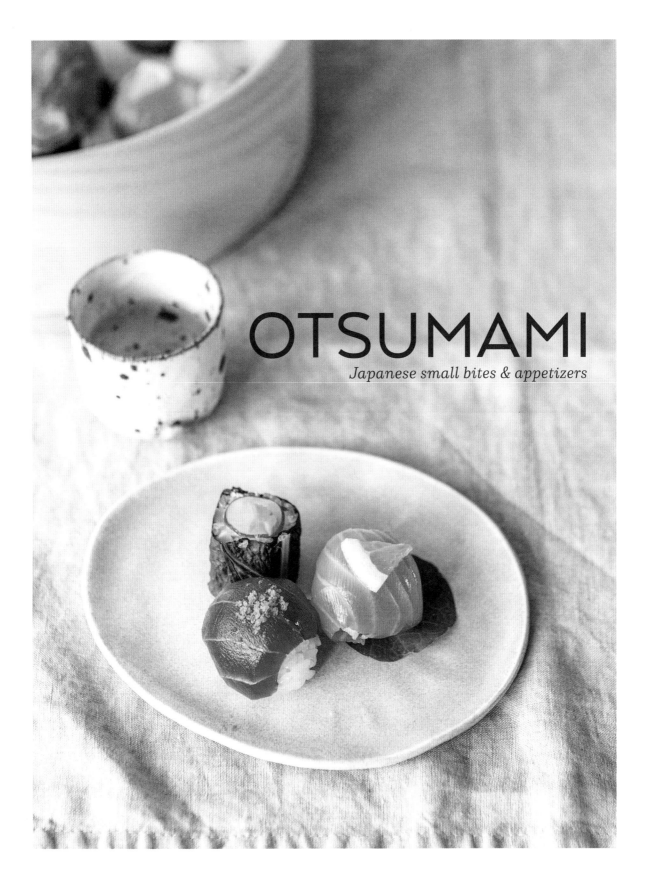

OTSUMAMI

Japanese small bites & appetizers

ATSUKO IKEDA

OTSUMAMI

Japanese small bites & appetizers

OVER 70 RECIPES TO ENJOY WITH DRINKS

PHOTOGRAPHY BY YUKI SUGIURA

RYLAND PETERS & SMALL
LONDON • NEW YORK

CONTENTS

WHAT IS OTSUMAMI?

The greatest pleasures in life are usually simple things. One of them is meeting with friends for a casual drink and a bite to eat. Whether at the pub, at a street-food market or at home, there is joy to be had in sharing downright delicious food from a selection of small plates, so that everyone can sample a taste of this and a bite of that. This unpretentious way of eating pairs perfectly with a drink.

Japan is famous for its otsumami, which means 'the nibbles you have while drinking'. Otsumami can come in many forms: hot or cold, raw or cooked, meat, fish or plant-based. All across Japan, you'll find different mouthwatering varieties of otsumami: whether in Fukuoka, jumping from one yatai (street food stall) to another, or walking through the Dotonbori district of Osaka chasing after the perfect takoyaki octopus ball or okonomiyaki pancake. The myriad of matsuri (festivals) throughout Japan are also celebrated for their street food, while it's always difficult not to order the whole menu at famous izakayas, the Japanese answer to tapas bars.

Inviting friends into your home for a relaxed gathering with drinks and nibbles always seems more daunting than it should. The difficult part being finding the right menu – you want something a bit different, that looks enticing and with enough variety in the dishes to keep everyone satisfied.

With this collection of recipes, I will help you surprise and impress your guests with some perfect otsumami food. Why not make some Rainbow Dips (see pages 56–57) to add splashes of colour to your table, or prepare some Blow-torched Salmon Belly Nigiri (see page 101) for your cocktail party? For a quick and easy fix, you could also make some Kimchi & Blue Cheese Gyoza Pizzas (see page 53). These are just a few examples of the scrumptious small plates and bite-sized delights on offer in this book. Infused with Japanese flavours, these dishes are all delicious, perfect for sharing, easy to make and beautifully presented.

Chapters are divided into Simple Light Bites, Meat & Poultry, Fish & Seafood, Vegetables and Tofu & Eggs to make it easier for you to navigate and choose your dishes. I've also added a section on party planning (see page 8), covering everything from designing your menu to kitchen and cooking prep. There is information about Furoshiki, the art of cloth wrapping (if you want to go the extra mile for an authentic Japanese experience), a basic guide to Japanese beverages and how to serve them, plus some deliciously inventive cocktail recipes to spice up your evening. With these tips, you'll soon become a pro at hosting and cooking for stress-free, delicious otsumami parties!

I hope this book will open your eyes to new possibilities in the joyful art of cooking and hosting, and that it can become a trusted companion which you go back to again and again…

PARTY PLANNING

A little advance planning will make your dinner party much easier to organize and eventually enjoy with your guests. To help you achieve this, here is a set of guidelines to consider before you get started.

A BALANCED MENU WITH A STAR DISH

Lay your menu foundation by first choosing your star dish or main course. To narrow down your options, take into consideration factors such as the fresh and seasonal produce available at the time, the weather or time of year, your guests' preferences and any food restrictions they might have.

Once you have chosen your star dish, you can start building the rest of your menu to support it. Japanese cuisine is all about balance and it follows what we call 'the rule of 5'. A meal should include:

5 DIFFERENT COLOURS (red, green, yellow, white and black/brown) for nutritional balance. Vegetables offer a wide variety of colours to choose from and sometimes only a touch of contrasting colour, such as from sesame seeds or spices, does the trick.

5 DIFFERENT TASTES (sweet, sour, salty, bitter and umami) to feel fully satisfied.

5 DIFFERENT COOKING METHODS (simmer, steam, fry, grill/broil and raw) for a variety of textures.

These rules might sound tedious to start with, but it's actually surprisingly easy to incorporate all these elements with a little planning! Contrasting and complementing are the key principles and will help you achieve a truly harmonious and delicious meal.

PLAN YOUR MENU

THINK SEASONAL

Seasonality or the use of fresh, seasonal ingredients, is at the core of Japanese cuisine and food culture. We even have a specific word, 'shun', which describes the exact moment when a vegetable is at its best, a fruit at its sweetest or a fish at its most flavourful.

In **SPRINGTIME** in Japan, we'll eat plenty of vegetables like cauliflower, watercress and lots of delicious seafood like Sake Steamed Clams (see page 118). It's also the time of year when we celebrate hanami or the tradition of cherry blossom viewing. It's all about meeting with friends under sakura trees, eating bentos and having a few drinks!

SUMMER DAYS in Japan are hot and humid so we gorge on thirst-quenching vegetables like cucumber, edamame or tomatoes. Cold or chilled dishes like cold noodle soup are popular for helping people beat the heat. It's also the time for matsuri festivals where yatai stalls serve their seasonal specialities like Takoyaki (see page 115) to festival-goers.

AUTUMN is the season of hearty appetites, just like the saying shokuyoku no aki says! It is really a feast of riches coming from the land with mushrooms and aubergine/eggplant, but also from the sea with mackerel and salmon, and from the sky with duck.

WINTERS are cold so we rely on hardy vegetables like potatoes and cabbages to keep us satisfied, as well as crabs to keep us nourished. Onions and garlic help to heat our bodies. Not to mention oysters, which are in season throughout the winter.

SEASONAL MEAL IDEAS

Eating seasonally makes a lot of sense: produce is at its freshest, cheapest and most nutritious when it arrives at the table... and your cooking can make a celebration of it! Of course, what is available seasonally will differ slightly depending on where in the world you live, so choose ingredients and dishes according to your location. You can also think about what will satisfy your guests needs according to each season.

春 SPRING
Your guests might be craving light, colourful food with fresh and zesty flavours. Chicken, seafood and vegetable-based dishes all fit the brief perfectly.

Cigarette Spring Rolls (see page 141)
Summer Rolls with Edible Flowers
   (see page 145)
Temari Sushi (see page 98)
Fried Chicken (see page 66)
Sake Steamed Clams (see page 118)

夏 SUMMER
Thirst-quenching cold dishes will go down a storm, as well as grilled recipes with charred, smoky flavours.

Miso & Chive Butter Corn (see page 130)
Grilled Scallops (see page 112)
Takoyaki (see page 115)
Edamame Peperoncino (see page 130)
Yakitori Grilled Chicken (see page 73)
Tomato, Basil & Ponzu Salad (see page 133)
Smacked Cucumber (see page 133)
Cold Miso Soup with Smoked Mackerel
   (see page 124)

秋 AUTUMN
A time for comfort food with plenty of umami and rich, earthy flavours. Recipes with mushrooms, as well as meat and fish with stronger flavours will be just perfect.

Aubergine/Eggplant with Sesame Soy Sauce
   (see page 134)
Mushroom & Miso Gratin (see page 148)
Marinated Fried Mackerel (See page 119)
Salmon Aburi Sushi (see page 101)
Duck Breast Nigiri (see page 81)

冬 WINTER
You want to offer your guests nourishing plates of warm, delicious food at this time of year. Hot pots, dumplings and rice dishes are all ideal choices.

Oysters with Daikon Sauce (see page 108)
Squid Dumplings (see page 111)
Grilled Sea bass (see page 123)
Kimchi & Tofu Hot Pot (see page 165)
Crab Meat Rice (see page 127)

PREP, PREP, PREP!

MAKE IN ADVANCE

Prep work is everything that can be done in advance
before the final cooking and serving of the meal,
essential if you (or your kitchen!) don't want to be
overwhelmed on the day of your party. A lot of dishes
can't be prepared completely ahead of time, but you
can usually follow the recipe up to a certain point.

· 2 days ahead of the party: sauces, pickles,
  cured fish or marinades can be made and
  stored appropriately.
· 1 day ahead of the party: dips or meat
  marinades can be made and kept in the fridge.
· On the day of the party: things like vegetable
  chopping and meat and fish seasoning can
  be done in the hours leading up to the party.

MISE EN PLACE

La mise, as they say in kitchens, is the French
culinary term for 'putting everything in place'. It's
about organizing and arranging all the ingredients in
your kitchen. Think of each dish you are making and
group all the ingredients needed for it together in one
place. Do this for all the dishes on your menu if you
can. This way you're less likely to forget an ingredient
(essential or presentational) at the end.

PREP YOUR KITCHEN

Organize your kitchen in such a way that all the
utensils or equipment needed to cook your dishes
at the time of your party, are in place and ready
to be used. This means putting the right pots and
pans on the stove, lining your oven racks with baking
parchment or foil, having your serving dishes and
cutlery within easy reach, etc.

SAMPLE MEAL PLAN

It can be helpful to write down the various meal components when planning a party. This way you can check you have a good balance of different foods – picking something from each chapter in this book is a good way to get started. Crucially, you can also see at a glance what needs to be prepared and when.

CHAPTER	RECIPE	PREP TO BE DONE 1–2 DAYS BEFORE	ON THE DAY PREP (2–3 HOURS BEFORE)	PREP AT THE PARTY
DRINKS			Beer and sake bottles in the fridge to chill	
SIMPLE LIGHT BITES	Cheeseboard (see page 47) Pickled Vegetables (see page 44)	Pickle the vegetables	Prepare the cheeseboard components	Serve on a large plate
FISH	Cured Sea Bass with Lime Ponzu Sauce and Truffle Oil (see page 107)	Cure the fish Make the sauce	Slice the fish and place on a serving dish. Cover and keep in the fridge	Pour the sauce over just before serving
TOFU	3 Cold Tofu Salads (see page 158)	Make sauce of your choice	Place the tofu on a serving dish, cover and keep in the fridge	Pour the sauce over just before serving
EGGS	Rolled Japanese Omelette (see page 169)	Make the sauce of your choice	Cook 30 minutes before the party	Serve warm with the sauce
VEGETABLES	Edamame with Chilli & Garlic (see page 130)		Cook 30 minutes before the party	Serve at the beginning of the meal
MEAT	Grilled Chicken Skewers (see page 73)	Make sauces: Yakitori sauce Tosazu sauce	Cut the ingredients and skewer them. Set aside in the fridge Prepare the cabbage	Cook and serve hot
RICE	Crab Meat Rice (see page 127)	Cook the rice	Make the soup base	Cook towards the end of the meal. Serve hot

WHAT TO DRINK
WITH FOOD

You may be wondering what beverages you can offer your guests that will perfectly offset the flavours of otsumami. Whether you go for beer, sake, shochu, whisky, a cocktail or something fruity with less alcohol, there is an option for every taste.

JAPANESE BEER

When arriving at an izakaya, the first thing we usually say when ordering is 'toriaezu biiru' or 'I'll start with beer!'. Beer is not a traditional beverage, but we love it so much that it accounts for two-thirds of the alcoholic consumption of the country! It complements traditional Japanese food well and we have a wide variety of pilsner-style lagers. The top three brands Asahi, Sapporo and Kirin are widely sold now in big supermarkets and Asian grocery stores.

HOW TO DRINK

For Japanese people, a beer should have a nice foamy head. Firstly, it looks more enticing and secondly, it tastes better! The foam prevents the beer from losing the flavour when oxygen reaches it, so try a foam to liquid ratio of 3:7 and see what you think!

Serving it in a chilled, frosty glass is also paramount. Japan has really hot temperatures and high humidity in summer, so a chilled beer in a frosty glass really hits the spot! For this, put your glass in the freezer for 30-60 minutes before pouring your drink or, if you have less time, fill your glass with cold water and ice cubes and put it in the freezer for 5-8 minutes.

NIHONSHU (SAKE)

What we call sake in Japan actually refers to any alcoholic spirit like whisky or shochu, etc. While 'nihonshu' refers to the traditional beverage you might know as 'sake', which is made from rice, water, koji and sometimes added brewer's alcohol. (FYI, the latter is not to make you drunk quicker, but to improve the flavours and to make it lighter!) Nihonshu has around 15-17% ABV, which makes it a little stronger than wine. Just like wine, choosing the right bottle for your taste can be a minefield if you don't know much about it. Very simply put, it's the rice polishing ratio (the lower it is, the more superior) and the type of brewing method that determine the qualities in nihonshu.

So, here are the six styles you should be aware of when choosing your tipple:

JUNMAI – the name means 'pure rice' and this variety has no added brewer's alcohol. It is typically fragrant with a rich, mellow flavour

HONJOZO – this is light, mildly fragrant and easy to drink

JUNNAI GINJO/GINJO – a premium sake with both fragrant and fresh notes

JUNMAI DAIGINJO/DAIGINJO – the most premium class of sake, this has a fragrant bouquet and an elegant, pure taste

HOW TO DRINK

Very broadly speaking, junmai daiginjo/daiginjo and junmai ginjo/ginjo, with their floral and fruity notes, are usually enjoyed chilled, while junmai and honjozo, with their broader range of versatility, can be served at a wider range of temperatures, from chilled to warm or room temperature.

Don't over-chill or overheat sake, though, or it will spoil the delicate flavour. The best way to warm it up is in a water bath to around 50°C (122°F); simply submerge your carafe or bottle in a saucepan of hot (not boiling!) water. If serving chilled, you'll want to cool it down to around 10C–15°C (50–60°F); to do this quickly, place the bottle in a bucket of ice for

30 minutes. Or if you have more time, keep the bottle in a fridge overnight and take it out to rest at room temperature 10–20 minutes before serving. Serving at this gently chilled temperature will draw out the delicate flavours and fine fragrances in refined sake.

If you are worried about having the right glassware to serve, no need to fret! For chilled or room temperature nihonshu, a wine glass (preferably for white wine) is just perfect. However, if you are serving it warm, avoid glass or metal vessels and choose a porcelain or ceramic cup instead.

SHOCHU

Shochu, not to be confused with its similar Korean counterpart, soju, is a traditional distilled alcohol that has been produced and consumed for over 500 years in Japan. It can be made with various ingredients, but the most common are sweet potato (imo), rice (kome) and barley (mugi). Because of this, its taste and aromas can vary greatly. You'll be surprised by its low ABV of 20–25% compared to other distilled alcohols. I'm not suggesting you should drink more of it though (!) although in Japan, we say shochu causes fewer hangovers than other alcohols. One explanation would be its low amount of acetaldehyde, but still, better not to drink the whole bottle!

HOW TO DRINK

NEAT – serve it at room temperature to really appreciate its taste

ON THE ROCKS – as the ice melts, the unique sweet smell of shochu really develops

CUT WITH WATER – either hot, oyuwari-style, for cold winter days (always pour the hot water first!) or cold, mizuwari-style, for a hot summer's day. The amount of water is up to you, but the general rule of thumb is a ratio of 6:4 shochu to water.

CUT WITH SODA WATER – known as sodawari-style, with a shochu to water ratio of 4:6. This is particularly refreshing, especially on a hot summer's day, and why not add a twist of lemon zest to it too?

JAPANESE WHISKY

For me, I used to think of whisky as something that dads drink, but when I tried Japanese whisky it completely changed my perspective. It has smooth, elegant and floral notes. Scottish whisky lovers must have been in shock when the Japanese single malt was named the best whisky in the world! But in fact, Japanese whiskies are deeply rooted in Scottish whisky traditions. The most famous brands are Nikka, Yamazaki and Hibiki.

HOW TO DRINK

Japanese whiskies are enjoyed like malt whiskies and in the same ways as shochu. My favourite way to drink Japanese whisky is in an old fashioned cocktail with sugar, bitters, water and orange zest. Whisky highballs are also a hugely popular accompaniment for otsumami dishes in Japan.

UMESHU/YUZUSHU

If you are not keen on drinks with a high alcohol content, then this option is perfect for you. These low-alcohol liqueurs (between 8–15%) are fresh, fruity, sweet and definitely mouth-watering! The most popular one is umeshu, which is made by steeping ume (Japanese plum) in liquor and sugar. The citrusy liqueur is called yuzushu, which is made with yuzu juice and zest, liquor and sugar.

HOW TO DRINK

You can either drink them neat in a chilled glass or on the rocks. The refreshing, tart taste makes these suitable for drinking as aperitifs before a meal.

COCKTAILS

There's a certain 'je ne sais quoi' about a cocktail... it feels slightly decadent and is delicious in its own right. Having one or two signature recipes up your sleeve is just what you need to ensure that your evening gets off to a flying start!

RASPBERRY MINT SHOCHU SLUSHY

100 g/3½ oz. frozen raspberries
100 ml/⅓ cup barley shochu
1 tbsp freshly squeezed lime juice
2 tbsp agave syrup
pinch of fresh mint leaves
200 g/7 oz. crushed ice

MAKES 2

Blitz all the ingredients, apart from ice cubes, in a blender or in a jug/pitcher using a hand-held stick blender to make a smoothie.

Strain the smoothie through a tea strainer or fine-mesh sieve/strainer and discard the raspberry seeds.

Pour the smoothie back into the jug/pitcher, then add the crushed ice and blitz again to make a 'slushy' texture. Serve in margarita glasses or coupes.

YUZU MARGARITA

60 ml/¼ cup shochu of your choice
   (ideally barley or rice)
60 ml/¼ cup yuzushu
   (yuzu liqueur)
2 tbsp Cointreau
1 tbsp freshly squeezed lime juice
pinch of salt
200 g/7 oz. ice cubes
1 tsp Campari

MAKES 2

Put all the ingredients, except the Campari, in a cocktail shaker and shake well. Strain the cocktail into two margarita glasses. Drop ½ tsp of Campari into each glass and let it sink to the bottom. Serve.

WHISKY GINGER

60 ml/¼ cup Japanese whisky
100 g/3½ oz. ice cubes
peel from 1 orange
120 ml/½ cup ginger beer

MAKES 1

Add the whiskey and ice cubes to a glass tumbler. Use heatproof tongs to hold the orange peel, then set it on fire and carefully drop it into the whisky.

Top up the drink with the ginger beer, then stir to combine and serve.

MATCHA SAKE

100 g/3½ oz. crushed ice
60 ml/¼ cup sake
2 tbsp freshly squeezed lemon juice
1 tbsp maple syrup
¼ tsp matcha powder
100 g/3½ oz. ice cubes
120 ml/½ cup sparkling water

MAKES 1

Put the crushed ice in a glass tumbler. Combine the rest of the ingredients in a cocktail shaker and shake well.

Strain the matcha sake through a tea strainer or fine metal sieve/strainer into the tumbler over the ice and serve.

From left to right starting on the previous page: Whisky Ginger, Matcha Sake, Raspberry Mint Shochu Slushy, Yuzu Margarita

FUROSHIKI

You most certainly know of origami, the traditional Japanese art of folding paper, but have you heard of furoshiki, the art of cloth wrapping? This simple but very useful skill will add a touch of Japanese authenticity to any occasion.

Equal parts beauty and function, furoshiki has been used in Japan for over 1000 years. The term actually refers to the square-shaped cloth used by people in the Nara period (710–794 AD) to wrap up their clothes to go to the public baths, hence its name furo 'bath', shiki 'spread'.

This astute way of carrying things quickly became popular for carrying other goods, like gifts and bottles, and remains so today. If you like watching anime, you'll notice Japanese school children and even adults on the way to work using furoshiki to carry their bento boxes! I also use it on a daily basis, whether for carrying my cooking tools to a class or wrapping up clothes before putting them in a suitcase. I love the practicality of it, and it looks so stylish too! Any fabric works and you can create furoshiki in all sorts of shapes and sizes depending on what is inside. Just like origami, the possibilities are endless!

Dubbed the first eco-bag, furoshiki is more relevant than ever in our environmentally conscious society. It is recyclable, multi-purpose and it exemplifies the Japanese philosophy of mottainai, or no-waste. So, time to get crafty and unearth your scrap fabrics and patterned cloths!

In the following steps, I will teach you how to use furoshiki to wrap bottles and bento boxes. It is such an elegant (and discreet!) way to carry them. It is perfect for bringing wine or food to a mochiyori (BYO) party, or for gifting items to your dinner party guests in a very personal and sustainable way.

You will need a 90 x 90-cm/35 x 35-inch cloth for wrapping two standard wine bottles of the same size, or square or rectangular bento boxes.

HOW TO WRAP
TWO BOTTLES

Place the furoshiki on a flat surface in front of you in a diamond shape with the inside of the cloth facing up.

Stand two bottles on the cloth next to each other and touching, slightly closer to the bottom corner. Carefully lay them down horizontally, with the corks/screw tops pointing outwards, leaving the natural gap between the base of the two bottles.

Tuck the bottom corner of the cloth over the bottles, then start rolling the bottles up in the cloth from the front to the back.

After rolling, bring both ends of the cloth into the centre, by standing the bottles up.

Tie both ends of the cloth together tightly. You can hold the part where it is tied as a handle.

HOW TO WRAP
BENTO BOXES

Place the furoshiki on a flat surface in front of you in a diamond shape with the inside of the cloth facing up.

Place the bento box in the middle of the cloth.

Fold the bottom corner of the cloth over and tuck it under the box.

Fold the opposite side of the cloth over the top to cover the box.

Fold both ends of the cloth together into the centre and tie them together tightly. You can hold the part where it is tied as a handle.

ESSENTIAL INGREDIENTS

Some of these ingredients, like panko breadcrumbs, tofu and miso, are usually readily available, even in smaller shops now. You may not come across some of the others every day, but they can be easily sourced in bigger supermarkets or Asian grocery stores. These ingredients are pictured from the top shelf left to right, then bottom shelf left to right on page 25.

SHIO KOJI (FERMENTED RICE AND SALT)

This all-purpose seasoning of fermented rice grains is made from rice, koji, salt and water. It has a mildly salty flavour and a subtle sweetness. I use shio koji for many recipes in this book, but it is especially useful for pickling and marinating as it tenderizes proteins (meat, fish and tofu). It is also very good for your gut.

PANKO (JAPANESE BREADCRUMBS)

With a much crispier and lighter texture than Western breadcrumbs, panko are often used for coating crispy katsu, stuffing patties and sprinkling on top of grilled/broiled bakes like the Mushroom & Miso Gratin (see page 148).

YUZU KOSHO (YUZU ZEST AND GREEN CHILLI PASTE)

Although fresh yuzu citrus fruits can still be hard to find in shops, you'll easily find yuzu kosho in Japanese grocery stores. This condiment is a mixture of yuzu zest, green chilli peppers and salt. It uplifts dishes and adds a slight heat to them. Just like wasabi, you only need to add a tiny bit of it. It tastes fantastic with Grilled Chicken Skewers (see page 73).

MISO (FERMENTED SOYBEAN PASTE)

Miso is a versatile seasoning and it can be combined with many other ingredients to create classic dishes or something new. Try some of the flavoured miso combos on pages 38–39.

SHIRO MISO (WHITE MISO)

This pale yellow, smooth miso is made only from soybeans and rice koji. The saltiness may vary in different brands, but it is generally mild and light in flavour. It's an extremely versatile miso, perfect in soups, marinades, dressings or even desserts.

AKA MISO (RED MISO)

Using the same ingredients as shiro miso, aka miso gets its darker colour and deep aromatic flavour from its longer fermentation period (over one year). Its texture can be smooth or grainy. Because of its stronger taste, it's perfect in sauces and stews.

GENMAI MISO (BROWN RICE MISO)

Made from soybeans and brown rice, it has a medium-rich flavour, but with all the great nutritional benefits of brown rice. This can be used in the same dishes as aka miso.

SHICHIMI (JAPANESE SPICE MIX)

A blend of seven ingredients, this typically consists of red chilli, sansho pepper, dried orange zest, black and white sesame seeds, hemp seeds and/or poppy seeds, green nori flakes and dried ginger. Sprinkle it on top of Smacked Cucumber (see page 133) and on Nikumiso (see page 63).

TOFU

Tofu is made of only three ingredients: soybeans, nigari (a coagulant) and at least 90% water. Depending on the recipe, water sometimes needs to be pressed out before using the tofu. It comes in different consistencies from soft to super-firm.

KATAKURIKO (POTATO STARCH)

A fine starch extracted from potatoes which has become more available in free-from stores. It is used to coat ingredients before frying, but it also thickens soups and sauces and binds ingredients for patties. It can be substituted with cornflour/cornstarch if needed.

KOMBU (DRIED KELP)

This is known as 'the king of seaweed' and packed full of flavour! Hence, it is used for making dashi stock (see pages 32–33), which is the base of many dishes. You can also use it to cure fish and make pickles.

SESAME SEEDS

Black and white sesame seeds are frequently used in Japanese cuisine. Big supermarkets now sell ready-toasted ones, but if you can't find any, raw ones work perfectly too. All you need to do is toast them yourself over low heat in a frying pan/skillet until fragrant. Be careful not to burn them though!

SAIKYO MISO (SWEET WHITE MISO)

This type of miso has a naturally sweet taste which comes from the rice. This elegant, sweet and salty paste is the most popular type of miso in Kyoto and is the miso of choice in the globally popular variations of miso-marinated fish dishes. It differs from other types of white miso in that it uses more rice koji, and the salt content is lower – typically around 5%.

SAKE/SHOCHU

(rice wine/distilled alcohol) (see pages 14–16)

JAPANESE MAYONNAISE

Kewpie mayonnaise is the most loved brand of mayo in Japan. Its delicious and distinctive taste comes from Kewpie's secret ingredient: its very own brewed apple malt vinegar, which creates a deeper, richer flavoured mayonnaise.

GOMA ABURA (TOASTED SESAME OIL)

This is commonly used in Chinese-inspired dishes such as dumplings and sauces. It has a wonderful nutty aroma. You can use it as it is or dilute it with a neutral oil. Note, there are two types of sesame oil: a toasted one and a raw one. In this book you will need the toasted version for all recipes.

YUZU KAJYU (YUZU CITRUS FRUIT JUICE)

The yuzu has an aromatic, tangy flavour that is distinct from any other citrus fruit. Like a cross between a grapefruit and a lime, it's essential in Yuzu Ponzu and I use it in Chicken Ramen Noodles (see page 86).

OKONOMIYAKI SAUCE

With the rising popularity of Japanese street food, this particular okonomiyaki sauce has become more accessible in recent years. The sauce is a kind of Japanese brown sauce, which is based on fruits, tomatoes, dates, vinegar, soy sauce, spices and mushrooms. The taste is mild and sweeter than brown sauce. It is not only served with okonomiyaki, but also goes well with takoyaki, burgers, and katsu (panko breaded fries). It is also suitable for vegans.

SHOYU (SOY SAUCE)

Made of fermented soybeans, wheat and salt, soy sauce is the most important seasoning in Japanese cuisine. Three kinds of soy sauce are used in Japan, but koikuchi (dark soy sauce) is by far the most common, and is therefore simply referred to as 'soy sauce' throughout this book.

USUKUCHI (LIGHT SOY SAUCE)

Usukuchi or light soy sauce has 2% more salt added than dark soy sauce, which has on average 16% saltiness. Hence, it tastes a bit saltier but is less fermented than dark soy sauce. Its paler colour won't darken the colour of your natural ingredients so much.

TAMARI SOY SAUCE

For a wheat-free option, choose tamari soy sauce which is gluten-free. It is traditionally the richest in texture and flavour.

MIRIN (SWEET RICE WINE)

Also called 'hon mirin' (real mirin), this sweet rice wine contains about 14% alcohol, and is used for seasoning many Japanese dishes such as yakitori, miso marinades, sauces and dressings. It is made from steamed mochi rice, rice koji (cultured rice) and alcohol. Its delicate, natural sweetness develops during the fermentation process. Hon mirin adds an elegant sweetness to your dishes. The finest quality mirin is called mikawa mirin. A less alcoholic (less than 1% of alcohol) option is also available.

KOME SU (RICE VINEGAR)

Rice vinegar is the most common vinegar in Japan, but brown rice or grain vinegars are also available. Rice vinegar has a mellow flavour, a low acidity (about 4.5 %) and is pale yellow in colour. It is an essential ingredient in sushi rice, gyoza dipping sauce and pickles.

RYORISHU (COOKING SAKE)

Just like wine in the West, sake can be enjoyed both as an alcoholic drink and used as a cooking ingredient. It tenderizes meat, adds an elegant flavour to dishes such as Sake Steamed Clams (see page 118). Specialist cooking sake is normally seasoned with 2% salt due to a taxation in Japan, but you can also find a no-added-salt version. If you aren't sure which one to use, always go for the basic quality option and you can warm leftovers up to drink as hot sake. There is not much difference price-wise.

AONORI (DRIED GREEN NORI FLAKES)

Also called green laver, this seaweed comes from the same family as the sea lettuce. It is a fragrant garnish, commonly used as a condiment for Okonomiyaki (see page 162) and Takoyaki (see page 115).

BONITO FLAKES (KATSUOBUSHI)

This umami-rich ingredient is most importantly used in making dashi stock (see pages 32–33). Katsuobushi comes from fermenting and smoking bonito (a type of tuna fish) which is then shaved into fine flakes. Because of its thin and airy texture, you can see it 'dancing' on top of dishes like okonomiyaki and takoyaki when served hot.

KOME (JAPANESE RICE)

See pages 30–31

KITCHEN TOOLS

Below is a list of tools you will find useful for making the recipes in this book. These tools are pictured on page 29, from the top shelf left to right, then bottom shelf left to right.

SEIRO (BAMBOO STEAMER)

This is a useful tool for steaming vegetables or dumplings. Steaming food in this way retains the flavours of the ingredients much better than boiling. Make sure your bamboo steamer fits snugly onto the saucepan you are using to avoid any steam escaping. There are several sizes of bamboo steamer available.

TEPPO GUSHI (SKEWERS)

Slightly thicker and stronger than other wooden skewers, these bamboo skewers have flat handles and are commonly used for barbecued meats such as Grilled Chicken Skewers (see page 73).

MAKISU (BAMBOO MAT)

An essential item for making rolled sushi of course, but a bamboo mat is also useful for wrapping dashimaki egg rolls (see page 169). After using this, you'll need to wash it thoroughly and then let the bamboo dry completely so it doesn't go mouldy when it is stored away (I put mine by a sunny window or on top of the radiator to dry during the winter time).

BENRINA (HAND-HELD MANDOLIN SLICER)

These are so well made that I have been using mine for over 18 years! It is a very clever tool that lets you easily slice vegetables as thinly as paper. If you invest in one, it will become your secret weapon for bringing a sophisticated look to the garnishes on your dishes. I use it to slice the root vegetables to make crisps on page 54.

OROSHIKI (JAPANESE GRATER)

This tool is the one my students search for online straight after my classes. It is useful for very finely grating ginger and garlic to make a paste. I have used it for many recipes in this cookbook. Oroshiki come in different materials, shapes and sizes; from small round ceramic versions to square stainless-steel graters. All produce very finely grated ingredients which give delicate flavour to dishes.

DOUGH CUTTER/SCRAPER

I use this all the time in my kitchen for transferring chopped vegetables to a bowl. It's so much easier and less messy than just using your hands! Just scoop the chopped veggies up with your dough cutter and the job is done!

SHIBORIKI (JUICE SQUEEZER)

If you make cocktails at home, this tool will help you keep your work surface dry. It can hold the juice of citrus fruit and fits very neatly in a drawer. I love Japanese design!

YASAI NUKIKI (VEGETABLE CUTTERS)

These cute little cutters add a seasonal touch to your dishes, with motifs in the shape of plants or animals depending on the season. They are mainly used to cut out shapes from hard vegetables such as carrots, daikon, radishes, beetroot/beet, etc. In this book, I have used them to make decoration for the Pink Soup recipe (see page 142).

TAKE GUSHI (BAMBOO SKEWERS)

Bamboo skewers make it easy to eat bite-sized food without using chopsticks or forks at your party. I use bamboo ones rather than plastic because they look elegant and are better for the environment. Plus, they can be washed and reused if they are not burnt or damaged. You can easily purchase these online nowadays.

RYOURI HASHI (COOKING CHOPSTICKS)

I use these a lot when I cook. Cooking chopsticks are around 28-30 cm/11-12 inches in length, so longer than regular eating chopsticks (usually 21-23 cm/8-9 inches). They are made of wood and great tools for beating eggs, picking up small things and deep-frying food. The other good thing about them is that they do not take up much space in the kitchen... but I seem to compensate for this by having multiple pairs of them!

MORITSUKE HASHI (SERVING CHOPSTICKS)

Not too dissimilar to tweezers, these chopsticks are essential for serving delicate dishes. As they are as thin as the tip of chopsticks, you will be able to pick up a grain of rice or clear some messy bits in your dish without damaging the shape of your final plate.

MOKUSEI SPOON (WOODEN SPOON)

I love wooden spoons, not only for stirring but for tasting soup or liquid as it is cooking. They do not transfer the heat so won't burn your lips like metal spoons.

YANAGIBA (SASHIMI KNIFE)

See How to Cut Salmon Sashimi on page 97.

TAMAGOYA KI (EGG FRYING PAN/SKILLET)

These pans are designed especially for making the rectangular rolled omelette, Dashimaki Tamago (see page 169). In this pan, thin layers of omelette are rolled into one long rectangular shape during the cooking process. Due to this particular cooking method, and the constant tilting of the pan during cooking, it is not suitable for use on induction hobs/stove-tops.

DONABE (JAPANESE HOT POT)

A traditional Japanese earthenware pot, donabes are useful for cooking hot pots, stews, soups and rice. Because they are made from a special type of clay, these pots can withstand high temperatures and can be set over an open flame (though they can't be used with electric or induction hobs/stove-tops). Donabes build heat slowly, just like a slow cooker. After the dish is cooked, we place the donabe on a round straw mat, to avoid burning the table, and serve the food straight from the pot.

SURIBACHI & SURIKOGI (PESTLE & MORTAR)

Suribachi literally means 'grinding-bowl' and surikogi translates to 'grind-powder-wood'. These are brilliant tools for grinding seeds, nuts or spices into a smooth paste. The difference between this and a pestle and mortar is the tiny grooves on the surface of the bowl, which really break down the ingredients. To use this properly, rub the stick repeatedly in one direction against the bowl without bashing it. Suribachi and sticks are sometimes sold separately, so make sure you get a suitable (larger in length) stick to go with your bowl. To clean, soak the bowl in hot water to loosen the ingredients that may be stuck between the grooves, then use a small brush to remove them.

HOW TO
COOK RICE

The defining feature of Japanese rice is its short, round grains, which become slightly sticky when cooked, making them easy to mould or pick up with chopsticks. Plain cooked Japanese rice can be turned into sushi rice with the addition of sushi vinegar seasoning (a mixture of vinegar, sugar and salt). Follow the steps below to make both versions.

WASH AND DRAIN

Put the rice in a sieve/strainer and rinse it under cold running water, stirring the rice with your fingers, until the water runs almost clear. Leave the rice to drain over a bowl or in the sink for 30 minutes – this will allow the grains to slowly absorb the water that remains on the surface, which will help it to cook evenly.

COOK

Add the rice and water (see right for amounts) to a heavy-bottomed saucepan and cover the pan with a lid (now don't uncover until the whole cooking process has finished). Bring to the boil over high heat. When you can hear the rice starting to boil, and see steam coming from underneath the lid, reduce to the lowest heat and simmer for the appropriate time (see right).

IF USING A GAS HOB/STOVE-TOP

If your cooker has four ring burners (as is usual in a domestic kitchen), then start by bringing the rice to the boil over the largest ring. If you have more than four ring burners, then use the second largest ring, which should be equivalent in size. Once it starts to boil, move the pan to the smallest ring burner and reduce the flame to the lowest setting. Simmer for the appropriate time.

IF USING AN ELECTRIC/AGA STOVE

The tricky thing about these appliances is that the burners/plates retain heat, so the temperature takes a while to reduce. For this reason, start the rice off over high heat, then once the rice starts to boil, move the pan to a different burner/plate on the lowest heat setting and simmer for the appropriate time.

IF USING AN INDUCTION HOB/STOVE-TOP

Induction hobs tend to be highly efficient and more powerful than standard cookers, so I would advise you don't use the highest heat setting for cooking rice. If your induction hob has 9 as its highest heat setting, bring the rice to the boil over 8, or one or two below your highest setting. Once it starts to boil, reduce the heat to about 4 (or the medium-low setting) on the same hob, then simmer for the appropriate time.

REST THE RICE

Remove the pan from the heat and leave the lid on for 10 minutes. After 10 minutes, the plain rice will be ready to use in your recipes like Crab Meat Rice (see page 127) and Curry Rice and Quail Egg Arancini (see page 172).

SEASON THE SUSHI RICE

To make the plain cooked rice into sushi rice, wet the surface of a mixing bowl and spatula to prevent the rice sticking. Turn the rice out into the bowl. Mix the rice vinegar, sugar and fine salt together in a jug/pitcher (see quantities to the right) to make the sushi vinegar. Pour the sushi vinegar over the rice and use the spatula to mix the rice gently.

COOL DOWN

Cover the rice with a clean, damp cloth and leave to cool at room temperature (do not put the rice in the fridge to cool or it will affect the texture). Body temperature rice can be moulded more easily than cold rice and tastes better with the toppings.

QUICK COOKING GUIDE FOR PLAIN RICE AND SUSHI RICE

COOKED RICE	400 g/14 oz.	800 g/1 lb. 12 oz.	1.2 kg/2 lb. 10 oz.
UNCOOKED RICE	200 g/7 oz.	400 g/14 oz.	600 g/1 lb. 5 oz.
WATER FOR SUSHI RICE	200 ml/generous ¾ cup	400 ml/1⅔ cups	600 ml/2½ cups
WATER FOR PLAIN RICE	240 ml/1 cup	480 ml/2 cups	720 ml/generous 3 cups
SIMMERING TIME (AFTER BOILING)	9 minutes	12 minutes	15 minutes
RESTING TIME	10 minutes	10 minutes	10 minutes

NOTE *If you are making sushi rice, add 10% more water than rice. For the plain rice, add 20% more water than rice for the correct consistency.*

QUANTITY GUIDE FOR SUSHI VINEGAR

COOKED RICE	400 g/14 oz.	800 g/1 lb. 12 oz.	1.2 kg/2 lb. 10 oz.
UNCOOKED RICE	200 g/7 oz.	400 g/14 oz.	600 g/1 lb. 5 oz.
RICE VINEGAR	30 ml/2 tbsp	60 ml/¼ cup	90 ml/⅓ cup
CASTER/GRANULATED SUGAR (UNREFINED)	1 tbsp	2 tbsp	3 tbsp
FINE SALT	½ tsp	1 tsp	1½ tsp

NOTE *If you're using a pre-made sushi vinegar, add about 10% of the amount of cooked rice. (If you want to work out how much you need before you start cooking, the cooked rice will weigh double the amount of the uncooked rice.)*

HOW TO MAKE DASHI

Dashi is an ingredient at the heart of Japanese cuisine, and is used as the base of many traditional dishes in this book. I have either specified which type of dashi to use, or I've left it up to you to choose your favourite for the recipe.

Dashi literally translates as 'to extract'. Unlike other kinds of broth, Japanese broth is mainly based on dried ingredients such as kombu, bonito flakes (katsuobushi) and shiitake mushrooms, which have delicate yet intense characteristically umami-rich flavours that can be extracted in a relatively short time. Thanks to the well-established ancient techniques of dashi-making, you will be surprised at how simple and quick it is to make proper dashi from scratch. Although, of course, like everything, instant powdered versions of dashi (or even dashi bags, like tea bags!) are available if you are short on time.

KOMBU DASHI

Kombu dashi is the favoured type of stock in shojin ryori (Buddhist vegan cuisine). Different varieties of kombu are available, each with slightly different flavours – Rishiri, Hidaka, Rausu and Makombu are the most common. There are two ways of making kombu dashi. Simply soak the kombu in cold water overnight to draw out its elegant flavour, or soak it quickly in heated water for a richer, deeper flavour. The recipe below is for the latter method:

1 litre/quart cold water
10 g/¼ oz. (5 x 10-cm/2 x 4-inch) piece of kombu

MAKES 1 LITRE/QUART

Place the water and kombu in a large saucepan and let it soak for at least 30 minutes.

After 30 minutes, start to gently bring the water to the boil over medium-high heat. Just before it reaches boiling point – when small bubbles appear at the bottom of the pan – remove the kombu and take the pan off the heat. The temperature should reach no more than about 60°C (140°F). Do not let the kombu boil; if you do the flavour will be spoilt. The kombu dashi is now ready to use. It will keep in the fridge in a sealed container for up to 3 days. You can use the same piece of kombu again to make another dashi, or dice and add it to soups or salads.

NOTE *The quality of water is as important for dashi as it is for brewing tea, so a soft or filtered water is ideal.*

KOMBU & SHIITAKE DASHI

This stock is useful in any vegetarian dish. The dried shiitake mushrooms add an extra earthy depth of flavour to the broth. The magic, umami-rich combination of both kombu and shiitake really enhances the flavour of any ingredient it pairs with. You can keep both the rehydrated shiitake mushrooms and kombu for use in other recipes.

1 litre/quart cold water
10 g/¼ oz. (5 x 10-cm/2 x 4-inch)
   piece of kombu
20 g/¾ oz. dried shiitake
   mushrooms

MAKES 800 ML/3⅓ CUPS

Place the water, kombu and shiitake mushrooms in a large saucepan and leave them to soak for at least 30 minutes.

After 30 minutes, start to gently bring the water to the boil over medium-high heat. Just before it reaches boiling point – when small bubbles appear at the bottom of the pan – remove the kombu. Do not let the kombu boil; if you do the flavour will be spoilt. Continue heating to bring the water and mushrooms to the boil.

Once boiling, reduce the heat to low and simmer, uncovered, for 10 minutes. Skim any scum off the surface of the dashi as it cooks.

Turn the heat off and strain the dashi through a muslin/cheesecloth or fine-mesh sieve/strainer. The dashi is now ready to use. It will keep in the fridge in a sealed container for up to 3 days.

NOTE *I wouldn't recommend freezing any dashi, it is easy to make and the flavours would not survive.*

KOMBU & KATSUOBUSHI DASHI

This is the most common dashi for non-vegetarians. It uses both kombu and bonito flakes (katsuobushi) together for an umami-rich dashi with a complex, deep flavour. It is perfect for clear soups, egg dishes or noodles in broth where the dashi shines through as the primary flavour.

1 litre/quart cold water
10 g/¼ oz. (5 x 10-cm/2 x 4-inch)
   piece of kombu
20 g/¾ oz. bonito flakes (katsuobushi)

MAKES 800 ML/3⅓ CUPS

Place the water and kombu in a large saucepan and leave to soak for at least 30 minutes.

After 30 minutes, start to gently bring the water to the boil over a medium-high heat. Just before it reaches boiling point – when small bubbles appear at the bottom of the pan – remove the kombu and continue heating. Once boiling, turn the heat off and sprinkle the katsuobushi (bonito flakes) into the kombu dashi. Leave to brew for 2 minutes, letting the flakes sink to the bottom of the pan.

Strain the dashi through a muslin/cheesecloth or fine-mesh sieve/strainer, letting it drip through. The finished dashi is now ready to use. It will keep in the fridge in a sealed container for up to 3 days.

SAUCES & DRESSINGS

These intensely flavourful sauces and dressings add umami oomph to milder tasting ingredients like vegetables, salad and tofu.

BANNO SAUCE

100 ml/⅓ cup mirin
1¼ tbsp sake
½ tbsp light brown soft sugar
10 g/⅓ oz. bonito flakes
100 ml/⅓ cup soy sauce

MAKES 200 ML/GENEROUS ¾ CUP

Put the mirin, sake and light brown sugar in a small saucepan and bring to the boil. Reduce the heat to low and add the bonito flakes and soy sauce. Simmer for 2 minutes, then leave to cool. Keep the sauce in a sealed jar or bottle in the fridge for up to a month.

HOW TO USE

This is a concentrated sauce, usually used for making noodle soup by diluting it 1:1 with water. It can also be used as a dipping sauce, or poured over a stir-fry or tofu dish (see page 158) or Agedashi Tofu (see page 166) and Dashimaki (see page 169).

From left to right: Onion Soy Dressing, Miso Ginger Dressing, Tosazu Sauce, Banno Sauce

MISO GINGER DRESSING

4 tbsp white miso
4 tbsp sesame oil
2 tbsp rice vinegar
2 tbsp mirin
1 tbsp maple syrup
¼ tsp peeled and finely grated fresh ginger

MAKES 200 ML/GENEROUS ¾ CUP

Combine all the ingredients in a jar or a bottle with a lid and shake well to combine. The dressing will keep in the fridge for up to a week.

HOW TO USE

This can be your everyday salad dressing. It goes particularly well with delicate salad dishes like the Torn Lettuce & Seaweed Salad (see page 154). It's also delicious poured over fresh or fried tofu.

TOSAZU SAUCE

90 ml/⅓ cup Dashi of your choice (see pages 32–33)
3 tbsp rice vinegar
3 tbsp mirin
3 tbsp light soy sauce

MAKES 225 ML/¾–1 CUP

Combine all the ingredients in a jar or a bottle with a lid and shake well to combine. The dressing will keep in the fridge for up to a week.

ONION SOY DRESSING

½ onion, grated
3½ tbsp soy sauce
3 tbsp mirin
2 tbsp rice vinegar
½ tbsp light brown soft sugar
1 tbsp freshly squeezed lemon juice
2 tbsp neutral oil such as vegetable or sunflower
1 tsp yuzu kosho (optional)

MAKES 200 ML/GENEROUS ¾ CUP

Combine all the ingredients in a jar or a bottle with a lid and shake well to combine. The dressing will keep in the fridge for up to a week.

HOW TO USE

This goes with basically everything! Yellowtail Carpaccio (see page 93), roasted veggies or leafy salad.

HOW TO USE

This can be used as an oil-free salad dressing with a seaweed salad, for example. In this book I've paired it with cabbage (see page 73) but it also works well with other marinated grilled vegetables.

TABERU LA-YU DRESSING

La-yu is a hot chilli oil originating from China and is the Japanese equivalent of the chilli infused olive oil found in pizza restaurants. However, La-yu contains more solid ingredients, hence the 'taberu', which translates as 'to eat'. You can pour this delicious dressing on top of fresh salad, silken tofu (see page 158), steamed fish or stir-fried vegetables.

100 ml/⅓ cup sunflower oil

30 g/1 oz. spring onion/scallion, roughly chopped

20 g/¾ oz. garlic cloves, thinly sliced

1 tbsp dried chilli flakes/hot red pepper flakes

10 g/⅓ oz. peeled and finely chopped fresh ginger

3½ tbsp toasted sesame oil

2 tbsp tamari or soy sauce

1 tbsp mirin

2 tbsp toasted white sesame seeds

30 g/1 oz. roasted peanuts, skinned, crushed

1 tbsp dried goji berries

1 tsp maple syrup

¼ tsp sea salt flakes

MAKES ABOUT 250 ML/1 CUP

Pour the sunflower oil into a saucepan and heat over medium heat. When the oil becomes hot (but not smoking hot), add the spring onion/scallion, garlic and dried chilli flakes/hot red pepper flakes. Fry over medium-low heat for about 10 minutes until they are light golden in colour. Take care that the ingredients do not burn and lower the heat if necessary. You are just looking to infuse the oil with flavour.

Turn the heat off. Prepare a heatproof glass or ceramic bowl with a cloth underneath to protect the worktop. Drain the hot oil into the heatproof bowl through a fine metal tea strainer or sieve/strainer. Set the bowl of oil and the sieve with the onion and garlic aside separately. Add the ginger to the oil while it is still hot – take care as it may sizzle in the residual heat.

When they have cooled slightly, transfer the fried garlic slices from the sieve to some kitchen paper and keep to one side, then discard the spring onion/scallion and chilli flakes/hot red pepper flakes.

When the oil has cooled down, add the toasted sesame oil, tamari or soy sauce, mirin, toasted sesame seeds, crushed peanuts, goji berries, maple syrup and sea salt flakes. You can use the fried garlic chips for a crunchy topping to your dish or stir them back into the oil if you prefer.

Leave the oil to rest for a minimum of 30 minutes to allow the flavours to infuse. Stir well before serving.

The dressing will keep in a sterilized jar for up to 2 weeks in the fridge.

MISO MUSTARD

MISO BUTTER

MISO HARISSA

FLAVOURED MISO

Miso is a seasoning so versatile that it can enhance the flavour of almost anything – from pesto to mustard! You can use these little flavour bombs as a cooking sauce, marinade or melt the miso butter over a hot dish to finish it. Keep these in the fridge and consume within 1 week.

MISO BUTTER

30 g/1 oz. unsalted butter, softened
1 tbsp white miso
1 tsp maple syrup

MAKES ABOUT 40 G/1½ OZ.

MISO MUSTARD

4 tbsp sweet white miso
2½ tbsp rice vinegar
1 tbsp agave syrup
1½ tsp Dijon mustard

MAKES ABOUT 100 G/3½ OZ.

MISO HARISSA

3 tbsp red miso
1 tbsp harissa
2 tsp maple syrup
2 tbsp olive oil
1 tbsp freshly squeezed lemon juice
½ tsp garlic purée/paste

MAKES ABOUT 120 G/4½ OZ.

MISO YUZU

MISO BASIL PASTE

MISO MAYO

MISO BASIL PASTE

30 g/1 oz. fresh basil, chopped
½ garlic clove, chopped
20 g/¾ oz. pine nuts, chopped
1½ tbsp extra virgin olive oil
½ tbsp freshly squeezed lemon
   juice
30 g/1 oz. white miso
½ tbsp maple syrup

MAKES ABOUT 120 G/4½ OZ.

MISO YUZU

3 tbsp sweet white miso
2 tsp mirin
1 tsp yuzu juice
¼ tsp finely grated yuzu or
   lemon zest

MAKES ABOUT 60 G/2 OZ.

MISO MAYO

3 tbsp mayonnaise
1½ tsp barley miso (or red miso)
½ tsp maple syrup (optional)

MAKES ABOUT 60 G/2 OZ.

Whiz the ingredients for the miso
basil paste in a food processor
or pound them in a pestle and
mortar. For the other recipes,
simply mix the ingredients
together.

SOY SAUCE &
SHICHIMI MAYO

YUZU MAYO

SMOKED
COD'S ROE MAYO

FLAVOURED MAYONNAISE

These delicious condiments are such an easy way of adding punchy flavour to your meals. Wasabi mayo is perfect with fish and seafood and the zing of yuzu mayo makes it the ideal accompaniment for fried foods. The truffle mayo can be your secret weapon for a touch of decadence.

SMOKED COD'S ROE MAYO

3 tbsp mayonnaise
30 g/1 oz. smoked cod's roe
1 tsp lemon juice

YUZU MAYO

3 tbsp mayonnaise
1½ tbsp yuzu juice
pinch of salt
pinch of grated yuzu zest

SOY SAUCE & SHICHIMI MAYO

3 tbsp mayonnaise
1 tbsp soy sauce
pinch of shichimi spice mix

UME MAYO

WASABI MAYO

TRUFFLE MAYO

TRUFFLE MAYO

3 tbsp mayonnaise
3 slices of fresh black truffle,
   finely chopped
a few drops of truffle oil (optional)

UME MAYO

3 tbsp mayonnaise
1 pickled umeboshi, finely chopped
   (or 1 tsp umeboshi paste)
pinch of golden caster/granulated
   sugar

WASABI MAYO

3 tbsp mayonnaise
2 tsp wasabi paste

**EACH MAKES AROUND
50–80 G/1¾–2¾ OZ.**

For each recipe, simply mix the
ingredients together in a small
bowl and serve. If you don't plan
on serving it straight away, keep
it in the fridge and consume within
3 days if using fresh mayonnaise
or a week if using store-bought
mayonnaise.

簡単な前菜
SIMPLE
LIGHT
BITES

OTSUKEMONO

A Japanese meal always contains tsukemono, or pickles. They say in Japan we pickle everything, which is mostly true. Try these and you'll understand why... and probably become addicted to pickles too!

PICKLED BEETROOT/BEET

250 g/9 oz. candy beetroots/beet
60 ml/¼ cup rice vinegar
2 tbsp caster/granulated sugar
⅔ tsp sea salt
juice from ½ passion fruit

SERVES 4

Peel the candy beetroots/beet and cut them in half lengthwise.

Mix all the rest of ingredients together in a small bowl, making sure the sugar and salt have dissolved.

Place the beetroots/beet into a resealable plastic bag and add the vinegar mixture, making sure all the surfaces of the beetroots/beets are immersed. Remove the air from the bag by dipping it into a bowl of cold water and seal immediately so it is almost vacuum-packed.

Refrigerate and leave to pickle for a minimum of 2 nights before draining and serving.

The pickled beetroots/beet will keep in the fridge for up to 1 week.

SHIO KOJI & VINEGAR RED RADISHES

250 g/9 oz. red radishes
2 tbsp grainy shio koji
1 tbsp mirin
2 tbsp rice vinegar
1 tbsp golden caster/granulated sugar

SERVES 4

Trim the top and root off the radishes.

Mix all the rest of ingredients together in a small bowl, making sure the sugar has dissolved.

Place the radishes in a resealable plastic bag and pour over the vinegar mixture, making sure all the radishes are immersed. Remove the air from the bag by dipping it into a bowl of cold water and seal immediately so it is almost vacuum-packed.

Refrigerate and leave to pickle for a minimum of 2 hours before draining and serving.

The pickled radishes will keep in the fridge for up to 1 week.

BABY CUCUMBERS ON SKEWERS

300 g/10½ oz. baby cucumbers
2 tbsp grainy shio koji
1 tbsp mirin
grated zest of ¼ lemon

mini bamboo skewers

SERVES 4

Peel the baby cucumbers lengthwise, leaving a few lines of skin on the cucumbers.

Mix the shio koji, mirin and lemon zest together in a small bowl.

Place the cucumbers in a resealable plastic bag and pour over the shio koji and mirin mixture, making sure all the vegetables are coated. Remove the air from the bag by dipping it into a bowl of cold water and seal immediately so it is almost vacuum-packed.

Refrigerate and leave to marinate for a minimum of 2 nights and drain before serving on skewers.

The pickled baby cucumbers will keep in the fridge for up to 1 week.

CARROT & DAIKON

1 carrot
10-cm/4-inch piece of daikon
dried kombu sheet, 5 x 5 cm/
    2 x 2 inches
peel from 1 lemon
75 ml/⅓ cup rice vinegar
2 tbsp caster/granulated sugar
1 tsp fine sea salt

SERVES 4

Peel the carrot and daikon, then cut them both in half lengthwise. If the carrot is a particularly large one, cut it in half across the width too.

Combine the kombu, lemon peel, vinegar, sugar and sea salt in a bowl with 2 tbsp water and mix well to dissolve the sugar and salt.

Place the daikon and carrot into a resealable plastic bag and pour over the vinegar mixture, making sure all the vegetables are immersed. Remove the air from the bag by dipping it into a bowl of cold water and seal immediately so it is almost vacuum-packed.

Refrigerate and leave to pickle for a minimum of 2 nights before serving. (For a quicker option, you could cut the vegetables up much smaller, about 1 cm/⅜ inch thick, and pickle for a minimum of 2 hours.)

Before serving, drain the pickling liquid and slice the lemon peel up into short strips to use as a garnish.

The pickled vegetables will keep in the fridge for up to 1 week.

MISO CUCUMBER

1 cucumber
½ tsp fine sea salt
3 tbsp white miso
2½ tbsp caster/granulated sugar
1 tbsp mirin
1 tbsp sake

SERVES 4

Peel the cucumber lengthwise, leaving a few lines of skin. Cut the cucumber in half lengthways, then cut the lengths widthways into four pieces. Rub the fine sea salt into the cucumber all over, then set aside for 20 minutes to draw out the excess moisture.

Mix all the remaining ingredients together in a small bowl, making sure the sugar and salt have fully dissolved.

Pat the excess water off the cucumber with kitchen paper. Place the cucumber pieces into a resealable plastic bag and add the miso mixture, moving the cucumber around with your hands inside the bag to make sure the cucumber is coated all over. Remove the air from the bag by dipping it into a bowl of cold water and seal immediately so it is almost vacuum-packed. Refrigerate and leave to pickle for a minimum of 2 nights before serving.

The cucumber will keep in the fridge for up to 1 week in the miso. Wipe off most of the miso before serving.

Both recipes pictured on page 45

CHEESE
MORIASWASE

自己流チーズの盛り合わせ
CHEESEBOARD (MY WAY)

I love it when there's a cheeseboard at a dinner or cocktail party. Sharing food with friends, family or co-workers makes the atmosphere so convivial and it's a great conversation starter. If you're a cheese-lover, you might raise an eyebrow at these combinations, but I promise you it will be worth trying something new!

BRIE CHEESE & WASABI SOY SAUCE

200 g/7 oz. brie wedge

TO SERVE
soy sauce
wasabi

SERVES 6

Slice the brie into bite-sized pieces. Serve with soy sauce and a little bit of wasabi for dipping. Just like you would for sashimi!

NORI & SLICED CHEESE SANDWICHES

3 nori sheets
6 cheese slices of your choice
   (9 x 9 cm/3½ x 3½ inches)

SERVES 6

Cut the nori sheets in half. Place the cheese on one side of half a nori sheet, then fold in half to sandwich the cheese in the middle. The size of the nori and cheese should match.

Serve straight away (otherwise the nori gets soggy). To make this into a canapé-style dish, cut the nori and cheese into bite-sized pieces and serve individually so your guests can help themselves.

SOFT CHEESE & PICKLED DAIKON

100 g/3½ oz. cream cheese
80 g/2¾ oz. Pickled Carrot & Daikon (see page 46) or shop-bought takuan, finely chopped
½ tsp ground black pepper, plus extra to serve
crackers, to serve

MAKES 10 BALLS

Mix the soft cheese, pickled daikon and black pepper together in a bowl. Place the mixture in the fridge for 30 minutes to set.

When you are ready to serve, roll the mixture into 10 small balls. Serve with extra black pepper and your favourite crackers.

SMOKED MACKEREL & CREAM CHEESE PÂTÉ

180 g/6½ oz. smoked mackerel (around 3 fillets), skin and any bones removed
200 g/7 oz. cream cheese
25 g/¾ oz. capers, finely chopped
40 g/1½ oz. gherkins, finely chopped
10 g/⅓ oz. fresh dill, finely chopped
grated zest of ½ lemon

TO SERVE
30 g/1 oz. fresh dill, finely chopped
crackers or fresh bread

MAKES 24 BALLS

Put the smoked mackerel fillets in a mixing bowl and mash them into flakes with a fork.

Add the soft cheese, chopped capers, gherkins, dill and lemon zest and mix together well. Put the mixture in the fridge for 30 minutes to set.

When you are ready to serve, roll the mixture into 24 small balls. Roll the balls in the chopped dill to coat them all over. Serve the mackerel pâté balls with crackers.

Pictured on pages 48–49

PROSCIUTTO MAKI SANSHU

Prosciutto e melone is one of the most popular Italian aperitivo with freshly prepared ripe melon. Here is my grilled/broiled version of prosciutto with fruits and vegetables. Prosciutto has a wonderful light texture and flavour, and the natural saltiness of the meat means there is no need to add extra salt to this dish.

6 asparagus spears, trimmed

200 g/7 oz. prosciutto or streaky bacon

1 peach, stoned/pitted, cut into 8 wedges

12 cherry tomatoes

a little olive oil, for frying and to serve

grated zest and freshly squeezed juice of ½ unwaxed lemon

6 x 10-cm/4-inch bamboo skewers, soaked in cold water for 15 minutes

ridged stove-top griddle pan/ grill pan

SERVES 4–6

Blanch the asparagus spears for 2 minutes in a large saucepan of boiling water. Immediately drain in a colander and rinse the asparagus under cold running water to stop the cooking process. Drain well again.

Tear the prosciutto lengthways into long ribbons and wrap each asparagus spear evenly with prosciutto along the stem, leaving the tip uncovered.

Wrap the peach wedges in two turns of prosciutto each.

Wrap each cherry tomato individually in prosciutto, then place two on each skewer.

Heat a ridged stove-top griddle pan/grill pan over high heat. Lightly oil the surface of the pan, then reduce the heat to medium-high.

Working in batches depending on the size of your pan, place the join of the wrapped prosciutto on the hot pan first to seal it, then cook for about 3 minutes, turning regularly until all sides are brown and crisp.

To serve, cut the asparagus diagonally into bite-sized pieces and place on a serving plate with the tomato skewers and peach wedges. Sprinkle with lemon zest and drizzle with lemon juice and olive oil to serve.

KIMCHI TO BLUE CHEESE NO PIZZA

キムチとブルーチーズのピザ

KIMCHI & BLUE CHEESE GYOZA PIZZAS

A real 'East meets West' recipe, I initially devised this one using leftover gyoza wrappers. I love how the wrappers become a pizza-like thin crust onto which I can slather some umami-rich toppings. My favourite is this unusual pairing of blue cheese and spicy kimchi: it shouldn't work but it does and it's incredible! The blue cheese actually offsets the strong kimchi flavour and adds a lot of tang. They're always a hit at parties and so quick to do.

10 store-bought gyoza wrappers
vegetable oil, for brushing
100 g/3½ oz. kimchi, drained and finely chopped
50 g/1¾ oz. blue cheese, crumbled
1 pear, thinly sliced into matchsticks

baking sheet lined with baking parchment

MAKES 10

Preheat the oven to 200°C/180°C fan (400°F) Gas 6.

Space the gyoza wrappers out evenly on the lined baking sheet.

Brush the surface of the wrappers with a little vegetable oil, then sprinkle each one with about 2 tsp kimchi and 1 tsp crumbled blue cheese.

Place the baking sheet on the top rack of the preheated oven and cook for 5–7 minutes until the edges of the gyoza wrappers turn golden brown.

Remove from the oven and garnish the pizzas with the thin slices of pear. Serve warm.

NEKKO YASAI NO AGEMONO

根っこ野菜の揚げ物
ROOT VEGETABLE CRISPS/CHIPS

Just by changing the way you cook them, humble vegetables can become such a popular snack. Crisps/chips are the perfect nibbles for pairing with drinks – especially in pubs, they are the go-to choice! Homemade crisps are fun, easy to make and the natural vibrant colours look fantastic. Plus, you don't feel guilty indulging in plenty of them knowing that, well... they're just vegetables!

250 g/9 oz. white potatoes
250 g/9 oz. sweet potatoes
200 g/7 oz. lotus root (if possible)
200 g/7 oz. red beetroots/beet and/or candy beetroot/beet
250 g/9 oz. parsnips
750 ml/3¼ cups vegetable oil, for frying

TO SERVE
Rainbow Dips (see page 56) or Flavoured Mayonnaise (see pages 40–41)

mandolin (if possible)

MAKES ABOUT 10 SERVINGS (450 G/1 LB.)

Wash the vegetables and dry them well. Keep the skins on.

Using a mandolin if you have one, thinly slice the potatoes, lotus root and beetroot/beet widthwise, across the fibre. Thinly slice the parsnips lengthwise, along the fibre. Most vegetables will shrink when they are deep-fried, so try to cut the slices as large (not thick) as possible.

Place the sliced vegetables on kitchen paper and pat dry on both sides.

Heat the vegetable oil in a heavy-based wok or saucepan to 180°C (350°F) over high heat. I use a 26-28-cm/10-11-inch wide wok-style pan, which allows the ingredients to spread out and not stick together. To test that the oil is hot enough, drop in a slice of potato. If it sizzles gently with bubbles around the ingredient, it is the right temperature. Reduce the heat to medium to maintain the temperature of the oil.

Start by frying the potatoes and finish by frying the beetroot/beet (which may colour the oil red). Working in batches, carefully drop a handful of vegetable slices into the oil. Don't touch the ingredients at the beginning, then when they start to turn golden, gently flip them over so they cook evenly. Most vegetables will take 5–7 minutes in total, but potatoes may take up to 10 minutes to turn golden brown. Keep a close eye on the vegetables as they fry, if any start to become brown all over it means they are overcooked.

Remove the crisps from the hot oil with a slotted spoon and drain well on a cooling rack. Some vegetables (such as carrots, parsnips and sweet potatoes) stay soft when you take them out of oil but will crisp up as they cool down.

Serve with your favourite dip or mayo. If you have any leftovers (not likely in my experience!) these will keep in an airtight container at room temperature until the next day.

NIJIIRO DIP

I love dips! A home cook's secret weapon – they're easy to make, can be prepared in advance and paired with infinite things. There is something so satisfying about dipping delicious food into something else to enhance it further. These recipes will delight your guests with their flavours and colours. The dips will keep in the fridge in an airtight container for up to 3 days. Each recipe makes 200–250 g/7–9 oz.

RED

2 red (bell) peppers
2 Romano peppers
3 garlic cloves, unpeeled
3 tbsp extra virgin olive oil
1 tbsp tomato purée/paste
½ tsp sea salt flakes
1 tsp baharat spice mix
30 g/1 oz. walnuts, finely diced

roasting pan, lined with foil

Preheat the grill/broiler to 200°C (400°F) or to medium-high.

Cut the red (bell) peppers and Romano peppers in half lengthways. Remove the stalks, seeds and white pith.

Place the peppers skin side-up in the lined roasting pan and lightly coat the skin of the peppers with 2 tbsp extra virgin olive oil. Add the garlic cloves next to the peppers.

Grill/broil for 20–25 minutes until the skins have blistered. Remove from the grill/broiler and leave until cool enough to handle.

Peel the peppers and discard the skin. Roughly dice the peppers and put them into a food processor. Squeeze the garlic out of its skin and add to the food processor.

Add the rest of the ingredients, apart from walnuts and remaining oil, and pulse to a smooth paste. Add the walnuts and mix well. Top the dip with the remaining extra virgin olive oil to serve.

PINK

2 tsp coriander seeds
1 egg yolk
90 ml/⅓ cup neutral oil such as vegetable or sunflower
100 g/3½ oz. smoked cod's roe, membrane removed
100 g/3½ oz. cooked beetroots/beet, puréed in a blender
2 tsp freshly squeezed lemon juice
¼ tsp grated garlic
¼ tsp sea salt flakes (optional)

Toast the coriander seeds in a dry frying pan/skillet over medium-low heat for 2 minutes. Grind the seeds to a fine powder in a spice grinder or using a pestle and mortar. Set aside.

Put the egg yolk in a bowl and beat with a hand-held electric whisk for 1 minute until the yolk is thickened and sticky. Beat in 1 tbsp oil to start with, then add another spoonful, beating until it is incorporated. Continue slowly beating in the rest of the oil – as the mixture thickens you can start adding it more quickly.

Add the cod's roe, beetroot/beet purée, lemon juice, garlic and toasted ground coriander seeds. Depending on the saltiness of the cod's roe, you can add the salt if you like.

ORANGE

250 g/9 oz. butternut squash
40 g/1½ oz. onion, cut into wedges
1 tbsp olive oil
¼ tsp sea salt flakes
1 tsp ras el hanout

Preheat the oven to 200°C/180°C fan (400°F) Gas 6.

Cut the squash in half lengthways and remove and discard the seeds. Dice the squash into 3-cm/1¼-inch cubes and place it on a baking sheet with the onion. Rub the oil into the vegetables, then bake in the oven for 15–20 minutes.

Leave to cool, then remove the skin from the squash. Place the roasted squash and onion in a food processor and blend to a smooth paste. Add the salt and ras el hanout, blend and serve.

GREEN

50 g/1¾ oz. fresh coriander/cilantro
1 garlic clove, peeled
75 ml/⅓ cup extra virgin olive oil
a pinch of salt
1 tsp fish sauce
1 tsp sweet chilli sauce
1 tbsp freshly squeezed lime juice
30 g/1 oz. cashew nuts

Place the coriander/cilantro and garlic clove in a food processor and pulse until finely chopped. Slowly add the extra virgin olive oil while the food processor is running. Stop the mixer and scrape down the sides using a rubber spatula.

Add the salt, fish sauce, sweet chilli sauce and lime juice. Add the cashew nuts, then pulse to make a chunky dip (I prefer a chunky texture but you can blend it further until smooth if you prefer).

BROWN

2 tbsp toasted sesame oil
250 g/9 oz. chestnut mushrooms, very finely chopped or pulsed in a food processor
2 garlic cloves, finely chopped
1 tbsp sake
1 tbsp mirin
2 tbsp red miso
1 tsp chilli oil

Heat a saucepan over medium heat. Add the toasted sesame oil, then fry the mushrooms and garlic for about 3–4 minutes until the mushrooms have softened.

Stir in the sake, mirin, miso and chilli oil and simmer for 2 more minutes. Leave to cool before serving or storing.

YELLOW

4 tbsp olive oil
40 g/1½ oz. onion, chopped
1 garlic clove, chopped
200 g/7 oz. medium-firm tofu, well drained, roughly chopped
2 tbsp light tahini
1 tbsp freshly squeezed lemon juice
½ tsp sea salt flakes
½ tsp ground turmeric
½ tsp English mustard

Heat a frying pan/skillet over high heat. Add the olive oil and fry the onion and garlic over low heat for about 7 minutes until softened.

Put the fried onion and garlic in a food processor and blend to a paste. Add the remaining ingredients, blend again until smooth and serve.

MAGURO NO YUKHOE

マグロのユッケ
*SPICY TUNA TARTARE
ON NORI CHIPS*

If you want to surprise and delight guests at a cocktail party, this dish is for you. These unusual little boats are actually nori chips holding spicy tuna tartare! The idea of the tartare came to me after eating the spicy Korean dish Yukhoe. Instead of using raw beef here, I use sashimi-grade tuna. I also mix the gochujang chilli paste with some mayo and pear to alleviate the heat.

300 g/10½ oz. sashimi-grade
    tuna loin
½ pear, peeled, cored and diced
    into small pieces
750 ml/3¼ cups vegetable oil,
    for frying

NORI CHIPS
3 nori sheets
2 tbsp katakuriko (potato starch)

CHILLI SAUCE
1½ tbsp gochujang chilli paste
1 tbsp soy sauce
2 tsp sake
pinch of light brown soft sugar
¼ tsp grated garlic
½ tbsp toasted sesame oil
1 tbsp mayonnaise

TO SERVE
10 g/⅓ oz. fresh chives,
    roughly chopped
1 tbsp toasted sesame seeds

28-cm/11-inch frying pan/skillet

MAKES 24

To make the nori chips, cut the nori sheets each into 4 equal squares, then roughly cut each square into two triangles. Set aside.

To make a light batter for the nori chips, combine the katakuriko with 100 ml/⅓ cup cold water cold water in a mixing bowl and stir. Set aside.

Put the vegetable oil in a heavy-based 28-cm/11-inch wide frying pan/skillet or wok over high heat and bring the temperature to 180°C (350°F). To test that the oil is hot enough, dip a nori chip in the batter and gently drop it into the hot oil. If it sizzles gently with bubbles around the ingredient, it is the right temperature. Reduce the heat to medium to maintain the oil temperature while you fry the nori chips.

One at a time, dip the nori triangles into the batter to evenly coat all over, then quickly but carefully drop into the hot oil from front to back (or away from you) to ensure you don't splash any oil on yourself. The nori chip will start sizzling quickly, as it contains water, but will dry within 10 seconds and be ready for turning. Turn it over to cook the other side for 20 seconds or until the bubbles disappear and the batter turns crispy. Remove the nori chip from the hot oil with a slotted spoon and leave to drain on a cooling rack. Repeat for the remaining nori triangles and batter. These cook quickly so you can cook one at a time or up to 4–5 in one go, just don't overcrowd the pan. The batter may separate if left out for a while, so just stir well before you dip the nori.

To make the tuna tartare, finely chop the tuna to a minced texture with a sharp knife, discarding any hard white sinew. Place the minced tuna and pear in a glass or metal bowl. Mix the chilli sauce ingredients together in a separate bowl, then pour the chilli sauce over the tuna and mix until well combined. Cover and keep the tartare in the fridge for at least 20 minutes and up to half a day until you are ready to serve. (Leaving it a little while helps the flavours to develop.)

Spread the spicy tuna tartare on the nori chips. Sprinkle with chopped chives and toasted sesame seeds and serve immediately.

HITOKUCHI CAPRESE

一口カプレーゼ
MINI CAPRESE SKEWERS

These little Caprese canapés are just so endearing! They remind me of mini Santa Claus, which is why they are perfect for a Christmas party. The addition of the miso to your pesto makes the flavours slightly rounder and warmer. Have fun putting these skewers together.

12 baby plum tomatoes on the vine
12 basil leaves
12 mini mozzarella cheese balls or 150 g/5¼ oz. mozzarella, diced into 12 bite-sized pieces
Miso Basil Paste (see page 39)

12 x 10-cm/4-inch bamboo skewers

MAKES 12

Use scissors to cut the tomatoes away from the vine, getting rid of as much of the vine as possible while still leaving the green sepals (leaves) attached to the tomatoes for presentation. Discard the vines.

Slice the top of the tomatoes with the green leaves off – these will be your little 'hats'. Thinly slice the bottom of the tomatoes off to stabilize them when they are placed on a flat surface. Skewer each tomato 'hat' on a bamboo skewer and push it right to the end. Set aside.

Place one of the 12 whole basil leaves on top of each whole tomato, then add a mini mozzarella or piece of diced mozzarella on top. Spoon a teaspoonful of the miso basil paste on top of the mozzarella, then carefully push the skewers through the little Caprese towers from the top to the bottom of the tomatoes. You should end up with the little tomato 'hats' on top.

Serve on a flat tray with napkins for a canapé party.

NIKUMISO

Nikumiso is traditionally miso mixed with minced/ground meat (niku), and it is used as a condiment or a topping. For this recipe, I added pearl barley to the meat for a healthier version. The taste of the barley goes particularly well with the red miso, but it also adds volume and a comforting chewiness to the dish. You can, of course, substitute the barley with other cooked grains, beans, lentils or quinoa. I like eating nikumiso on top of some rice or tofu, or even wrapped in lettuce leaves. In this recipe, I use it in a slightly more elegant way: served on chicory/endive 'boats' – it's the perfect mess-free canapé!

50 g/1¾ oz. leek, white part only (the green part can be used to make stock/broth)
1 tbsp vegetable oil
10 g/⅓ oz. peeled and finely chopped fresh ginger
250 g/8 oz. minced/ground beef
80 g/2¾ oz. cooked pearl barley
2 tbsp sake
3 tbsp red miso
2 tbsp mirin
1 tbsp light brown soft sugar

TO SERVE
2 red or green chicories/endive
shichimi spice mix

SERVES 6

Remove the outer layer of the leek if it is dry. Reserve the top 5 cm/2 inches of white leek for the garnish. Cut it lengthwise into thin slices and leave to soak in cold water to remove the bitterness.

Leaving the root still attached, thinly slice the remaining leek lengthwise so it doesn't fall apart, then cut across in the opposite direction to very finely chop.

Heat a frying pan/skillet over medium heat. Add the oil to the pan, then fry the chopped leek and ginger for 2 minutes, stirring constantly.

Add the beef to the pan and break up the lumps of meat using a spatula. Cook until the meat is all browned, then add the cooked pearl barley, sake, red miso, mirin and brown sugar. Stir continuously while cooking for 2 minutes until the liquid has evaporated. Remove the mixture from the heat, tip into a bowl and leave to cool a little.

Slice the root off the chicory/endive and peel apart the petals or 'boats'. Slice the bottom of the outer side of each chicory/endive leaf to stabilize it so it won't be wobbly.

Spoon the beef and pearl barley mixture into the chicory/endive boats. Drain the soaked leek and use it to garnish the dish along with a sprinkle of shichimi spice mix.

NOTE *This dish is best served when the nikumiso is at room temperature. When it gets cold the fat in the meat will solidify, so heat it through again well before cooling slightly and serving.*

肉と鳥肉
MEAT & POULTRY

KARAAGE

Karaage needs no introduction anymore! What makes Japanese fried chicken so special is the marinade in which the chicken is coated before cooking. It makes it exceptionally flavourful and juicy, while the coating stays extra crispy. My secret ingredient for this is shio koji, a natural seasoning used in Japanese cooking that tenderizes and enhances the umami in foods. It is made of three simple ingredients: water, salt and rice koji.

600 g/1 lb. 5 oz. skin-on, boneless chicken thighs

60 g/scant ⅔ cup katakuriko (potato starch) or cornflour/cornstarch

60 g/scant ½ cup plain/all-purpose flour

500 ml/2 cups plus 2 tbsp vegetable oil, for deep-frying

freshly squeezed juice of ½ lime or lemon, to serve

MARINADE
60 g/2 oz. shio koji (10% of the weight of chicken)
2 tbsp sake
1 garlic clove, grated

NEGI SAUCE
60 g/2 oz. leek
4 tbsp soy sauce
2 tbsp rice vinegar
2 tbsp light brown soft sugar

SERVES 4-6

To even out the thickness and help them cook evenly and quickly, place the chicken thighs skin side down and score the thickest parts of the flesh (about 1–2 cm/⅓–¾ inch deep) on either side of the thighs.

Mix the marinade ingredients together in a large bowl, add the chicken and stir to coat in the marinade.

Cover the bowl and refrigerate ideally for at least 2 hours or overnight. (If you are in a rush, a speedy option is to dice the chicken up into small pieces and marinate it for 30 minutes.)

Meanwhile, make the negi sauce. Trim the green end of the leek, then thinly slice the leek lengthways while the root is still attached. Finely chop the leek widthways across the previous slices. Put the soy sauce, rice vinegar and brown sugar in a mixing bowl and stir together. Add the finely chopped leek and set aside for at least 20 minutes for the leek to soak up all the flavours.

Mix together the katakuriko (potato starch) or cornflour/cornstarch and plain/all-purpose flour in a mixing bowl. Toss the marinated meat in the flour mixture to coat on all sides.

Heat the vegetable oil in a heavy-based saucepan to 170°C (340°F) over high heat. To check that the oil is ready, drop in a small piece of batter (made out of a mixture of the flour and marinade). If it sinks halfway and then floats to the surface and sizzles, then it means the oil is ready. Reduce the heat to medium to maintain the temperature.

Deep-fry the chicken, two pieces at a time, for about 6–10 minutes (depending on the thickness of the meat) per batch, turning over a few times in the oil until crispy.

Remove with a slotted spoon and drain on a cooling rack while you fry the rest. Cut into the thickest part of the chicken to check that the meat is cooked through. If it is pink, put it back in the oil for another 2 minutes.

Serve the crispy chicken hot with the negi sauce poured over it and a squeeze of fresh lemon or lime juice.

TORITEBASAKI BALSAMICO AJI

鶏手羽先バルサミコ味
BALSAMIC CHICKEN WINGS

There's nothing more comforting and satisfying than sitting across a plate full of glazed chicken wings ready to be picked apart with your fingers, whether you're amongst friends or alone! Chicken wings or tebasaki are a hugely popular dish in Nagoya where they are coated in a peppery glaze. In my recipe, I prefer to keep the heat out but I add some balsamic vinegar for a moreish sweet and sour taste. Let's see now if you can pick up the skills of Nagoya residents who are famous for eating them without leaving any meat on the bones!

750 g/1 lb. 10 oz. chicken wings
40 g/generous ¼ cup plain/
    all-purpose flour
750 ml/3¼ cups vegetable oil,
    for frying
fine salt and freshly ground black
    pepper
2 tbsp white sesame seeds, to serve

AMAGARA SAUCE
2 tbsp sake
2 tbsp mirin
2 tbsp soy sauce
1 tbsp balsamic vinegar
2 tsp light brown soft sugar
1 tsp garlic purée/paste
1 tsp Tobanjan
    (Chinese chilli bean paste)

SERVES 4

Wipe off any excess water from the chicken wings with kitchen paper and season them with salt and pepper. Coat the chicken wings in flour all over, then set aside.

Heat the vegetable oil in a heavy-based saucepan to 170°C (340°F) over high heat.

To check that the oil is ready, stick the end of a wooden cooking chopstick (or wooden spatula) into the oil. If it creates bubbles around the utensil, your oil is ready for frying. If it is bubbling hard, the oil is too hot; let it cool a bit and check the temperature again. Once the correct temperature has been reached, reduce the heat to medium to maintain it.

Add the chicken wings, 6 pieces at a time, and deep-fry for about 10 minutes per batch, turning over a few times in the oil until golden brown. When each batch is cooked, use a slotted spoon to transfer the wings from the hot oil to a cooling rack to drain the oil.

To make the amagara sauce, add all the ingredients along with 60 ml/ ¼ cup water to a large frying pan/skillet, stir to combine them and bring to the boil. Once boiling, reduce the heat to medium. Add all the fried chicken wings to the pan and turn them over a few times to coat in the sauce until sticky and slightly caramelized all over.

Tip the chicken wings out onto a large serving plate and sprinkle with sesame seeds to serve.

GYU NO TATAKI SALADA

牛のたたきサラダ
SEARED BEEF SALAD

Tataki refers to the traditional cooking technique of flash-searing a piece of meat (or fish) over scorching heat and leaving its centre very rare. It is then thinly sliced and served with a dressing. In this recipe, I make a sesame and cider dressing. It's warm, well-rounded in flavour and goes wonderfully well with the meltingly tender rare beef. A real treat for meat-lovers!

300 g/10½ oz. fillet of beef
   (e.g. 10-cm/4-inch diameter,
   5-cm/2-inch length or skinny
   and long would be ideal)
1 tbsp olive oil
1 red onion, very thinly sliced
2 spring onions/scallions, cut into
   5-cm/2-inch lengths, thinly sliced
   lengthways
100 ml/⅓ cup vegetable oil,
   for shallow-frying
200 g/7 oz. mixed leaf salad
   (such as baby leaves and rocket/
   arugula)
60 g/2 oz. grated daikon, excess
   water squeezed out

SESAME & CIDER DRESSING
3 tbsp light tahini
3 tbsp light soy sauce
3 tbsp mirin
2 tbsp apple cider vinegar
¼ tsp grated garlic

SERVES 4

Take the beef fillet out of the fridge 30 minutes before cooking to bring it to room temperature.

Preheat the oven to 200°C/180°C fan (400°F) Gas 6.

Heat a large frying pan/skillet over medium heat. Rub the olive oil all over the beef, then fry in the hot pan for 10 minutes, turning occasionally, until the outside of the meat is evenly browned.

Transfer the beef to a roasting pan, then put it on the middle rack in the preheated oven to roast for about 5–10 minutes, depending on the thickness of the beef, until medium-rare. Remove from the oven and leave to rest for 10 minutes before slicing.

Meanwhile, put the red onion to soak in a small bowl of water for 10 minutes to remove the bitterness. Drain well.

To make the sesame and cider dressing, put the light tahini and light soy sauce in a clean jar with a lid, then shake hard until the mixture becomes smooth. (Do not put all the dressing ingredients in in one go otherwise it will separate.) Next, add the mirin and shake well until combined. Add the apple cider vinegar and grated garlic and shake again. The dressing should become thicker when the vinegar has been added. Set aside.

When the beef has rested, thinly slice it across the grain. Set the sliced beef aside for up to 5 minutes and the colour will grow brighter as it is exposed to the air.

Meanwhile, shallow-fry the spring onions/scallions in the oil for about 5 minutes over medium-low heat until golden brown and crispy. Use a slotted spoon to transfer the fried onions to kitchen paper to drain the oil.

Put the sliced beef on a serving plate and scatter over the salad leaves and grated daikon. Drizzle with the sesame and cider dressing and garnish with the red onion and crispy spring onions/scallions.

YAKITORI

焼き鳥
GRILLED CHICKEN SKEWERS

Yakitori are such a popular otsumami in Japan. You'll find them in izakayas, street festivals, yatai foodstalls, grab 'n' go sections of supermarkets, and they also have their very own joints, yakitori-ya. While yakitori are not typically made at home, they're actually such an easy dish to prepare – it's essentially grilled/broiled chicken skewers with a sweet basting sauce. It's the sauce that makes them so delicious.

650 g/1 lb. 7 oz. skin-on boneless chicken thighs, diced into bite-sized pieces (you should get 4–6 pieces from one thigh)

4 spring onions/scallions or baby leeks, cut into 3-cm/1¼-inch lengths

6 fresh shiitake mushrooms, stems removed and halved

1 tbsp vegetable oil, for frying

shichimi spice mix and/or yuzu kosho, to serve

YAKITORI SAUCE
60 ml/¼ cup soy sauce
30 ml/2 tbsp mirin
30 ml/2 tbsp sake
1 tbsp light brown soft sugar

CABBAGE WITH TOSAZU SAUCE
sweetheart (pointy) cabbage, root and outer leaves removed, torn into bite-sized pieces
Tosazu Sauce (see page 35)

12 wooden skewers (roughly 15 cm/6 inches long), soaked in cold water for 15 minutes

MAKES 12 SKEWERS

Soak the cabbage in a bowl of cold water for 10 minutes, then drain well and keep in the fridge until you are ready to serve it.

To make the yakitori sauce, combine the soy sauce, mirin, sake and brown sugar in a small saucepan. Simmer over medium-low heat for about 8 minutes, stirring occasionally, until slightly thickened. Set aside.

Thread each soaked wooden skewer with a piece of spring onion/scallion, followed by a piece of chicken with the skin side facing outwards (rather than towards the ingredient next to it). Repeat the same process once more for each skewer, and finish each skewer with a slice of shiitake mushroom. Turn the skin of the chicken to the same side on each skewer so you can cook the skin side first to draw the fat out of it.

To fry the yakitori, heat a large frying pan/skillet over high heat. Add ½ tbsp vegetable oil, then put six of the skewers, skin side-down, into the pan. Turn the heat down to medium and fry for about 5 minutes. Carefully remove most of the fat from the pan with a piece of kitchen paper held in tongs. Turn the skewers over and cook the other side for 3 more minutes.

Pour half of the yakitori sauce over the chicken skewers, then simmer for about 2 minutes until caramelized. Turn the skewers in the sauce to make sure all the ingredients are coated. Remove the skewers to a plate and repeat the cooking process with the remaining skewers and yakitori sauce.

Alternatively, you can grill/broil the skewers if you prefer: preheat the grill/broiler to 200°C (400°F) or to medium-high. Place the skewers on a grill/broiler pan with a rim and grill/broil for 10 minutes. Brush the yakitori sauce over the chicken, then grill/broil for another 10 minutes, brushing them with more sauce and turning them a couple more times as they cook. Heat the remaining yakitori sauce in a small saucepan and simmer for 5 minutes until thickened and hot to serve alongside the chicken.

Place the cabbage on a large serving plate, then pour the tosazu all over the cabbage. Serve alongside the hot chicken yakitori with shichimi spice mix and/or yuzu kosho.

WAFU ANKAKE MEATLOAF

和風あんかけミートローフ
和風あんかけミートローフ
MEATLOAF WITH ANKAKE SAUCE

Meatloaves are a delicious and easy way to feed a bigger group of people. I like to place some eggs and okra in the middle, so when sliced, it looks incredible. Don't miss the ankake sauce step – it really brings it to the next level. It keeps the meatloaf moist and its savoury flavour really adds oomph the dish!

6 eggs
a little plain/all-purpose flour,
    for dusting
500 g/1 lb. 2 oz. minced/ground
    pork
250 g/9 oz. minced/ground beef
3 tbsp red miso
1 tbsp muscovado sugar
½ tsp salt
½ tsp ground black pepper
1 onion, finely chopped
50 g/1¾ oz. panko breadcrumbs
6 okra
20 g/¾ oz. white sesame seeds
3 tbsp aonori seaweed flakes
English mustard, to serve

ANKAKE SAUCE
100 ml/⅓ cup soy sauce
100 ml/⅓ cup mirin
100 ml/⅓ cup sake
2½ tbsp muscovado/dark brown
    sugar
1½ tbsp katakuriko (potato starch),
    mixed with 1½ tbsp cold water
    in a cup

10 x 20-cm/4 x 8-inch loaf pan,
lined with baking parchment

SERVES 8

Preheat the oven to 200°C/180°C fan (400°F) Gas 6.

Bring 1.5 litres/quarts water to the boil in a medium saucepan. Carefully add four of the eggs, stir gently to centre the yolks, then leave to boil for exactly 7 minutes for soft-boiled/soft-cooked. Transfer the eggs to a bowl of cold water to stop the cooking process and leave for 5 minutes. Gently peel the eggs, then dust them with a little flour and set aside.

Put the pork and beef in a mixing bowl with the miso, muscovado sugar, salt and pepper and mix until smooth. Add the onion, remaining 2 eggs and panko breadcrumbs and mix until combined.

Spread a quarter of the meat mixture evenly into the bottom of the prepared loaf pan. Place the boiled eggs in a row down the middle of the pan, then add some more meat mixture on either side. Place the okra beside the eggs lengthwise, then top with the rest of the meat mixture to cover and fill any gaps. Spread the surface flat and sprinkle with sesame seeds on one side and aonori seaweed flakes on the other side (you can use a sheet of paper to cover one side as you sprinkle to get a neat look).

Bake the meatloaf in the preheated oven for 45 minutes.

Poke a skewer into the centre of the loaf to check whether it is cooked. The liquid that comes out of the hole should be clear. If it is cloudy then put it back in the oven for 5 minutes before checking again. Discard any excess fat and juice that has come out of the loaf, then leave to cool in the pan.

Meanwhile, make the ankake sauce. Bring the soy sauce, mirin, sake and muscovado sugar to the boil in a saucepan. Reduce the heat to low, mix the katakuriko and water mixture well, then slowly stir it into the ankake sauce to thicken. Bring to the boil again, then remove from the heat.

Leave the meatloaf to cool, then remove from the pan and slice into portions. Serve with the ankake sauce and English mustard.

KATSU SANDO

カツサンド
BREADED PORK CUTLET SANDWICHES

Katsu sando, as we call it in Japan, is our star sandwich: fried crispy panko-crusted pork cutlets, dressed with tangy tonkatsu sauce, topped with crunchy gem lettuce and encased in two soft slices of white bread. Everything works so well together here, it's no surprise the katsu sando is becoming hugely popular outside of Japan!

PORK KATSU

2 thick pork loin steaks
   (roughly 2 cm/¾ inch thick)
30 g/3⅔ tbsp plain/all-purpose
   flour
1 egg, beaten
60 g/1⅓ cups panko breadcrumbs
750 ml/3¼ cups rapeseed/canola
   oil or vegetable oil, for frying
salt and freshly ground black pepper

TO SERVE

80 g/2¾ oz. white or green cabbage
2 tbsp English mustard
4 slices of extra-thick white bread,
   toasted on one side for extra
   crunch
4 tbsp tonkatsu sauce
pickles (such as gherkins and
   baby onions)

MAKES 8 BITE-SIZED SANDWICHES

Score both pork loin steaks at 2.5-cm/1-inch intervals where the fat and meat connect, this will help stop the meat from curling up as it cooks.

Put the flour, beaten egg and panko breadcrumbs on three separate plates. Season the pork steaks with salt and pepper, then dip both sides into the flour, then the beaten egg, then the panko breadcrumbs, ensuring an even coating on both sides. Refrigerate the pork loins for 15 minutes to set the coating.

Meanwhile, thinly slice the cabbage (I like to use a mandolin Japanese slicer), then soak the slices of cabbage in a bowl of cold water for 10 minutes to keep the texture crisp. Drain well.

To deep-fry the pork katsu, heat the oil in a heavy-based saucepan to 170°C (340°F) over high heat. To check that the oil is ready, drop a few panko breadcrumbs into the oil. If they float to the surface and gently sizzle, the oil is ready. Once the correct temperature has been reached, reduce the heat to medium.

Deep-fry each katsu one at a time for 7–10 minutes (depending on the thickness of the pork), turning over a few times until golden brown. Remove the pork from the oil with a slotted spoon and leave on a cooling rack with a tray underneath for the oil to drain for 5 minutes. This will also help the katsu to continue cooking with the remaining heat.

To assemble the sandos, spread a thin layer of mustard on the toasted side of two slices of bread, followed by a generous layer of tonkatsu sauce. Place a pork cutlet on top of each slice of bread and slather again with tonkatsu sauce. Divide the cabbage between the sandwiches, then top with the remaining slices of bread (toasted side in).

Wrap the sandwiches in baking parchment or tin foil, then put a weight (such as a heavy baking sheet) on top and leave for 10 minutes.

Unwrap the sandwiches, then cut the crusts off for a Japanese look (or keep the crusts on if you prefer), then cut each sandwich in half. To make finger-food versions, cut the sandwiches into quarters and use skewers to hold them together. Serve with pickled gherkins and baby onions.

LAMB MISO HARISSA YAKI

ラムみそハリッサ焼き
*GRILLED MISO HARISSA
RACK OF LAMB*

Apart from in Hokkaido where people can enjoy the traditional Gengis Khan mutton stew, sheep's meat has never really been part of a Japanese diet. It's only since moving to the UK and tasting British lamb that I have fallen in love with this rich and delicious meat. This recipe is a real showstopper when having friends over: not only does it look sumptuous, but it tastes absolutely delicious. Inspired by Middle Eastern cuisine and its love of lamb, harissa is here mixed with miso to make an aromatic umami bomb! You can replace the lamb with aubergine/eggplant or cauliflower as a vegetarian/vegan option.

500 g/1 lb. 2 oz. French-trimmed rack of lamb (8 chops)
1 tsp olive oil
Miso Harissa Sauce (see page 38)

TO GARNISH
100 g/3½ oz. watercress
25 g/¾ oz. pomegranate seeds

MAKES 8

If your lamb comes in a vacuum-sealed pack, take it out and let the meat breathe for a day in the fridge. The next day, 30 minutes before cooking the lamb, take it out of the fridge to bring it to room temperature.

Preheat the oven to 200°C/180°C fan (400°F) Gas 6.

Rub the olive oil all over the lamb. Heat a large frying pan/skillet over medium heat. When the pan is hot, add the lamb and fry for 10 minutes to brown the outside.

Place the lamb rack, ribs side-up in a roasting pan. Put the pan on the middle shelf in the preheated oven to roast for 10–15 minutes for medium-rare (leaving it for a little more or less time within this range depending on the size of your piece of meat).

Towards the end of the roasting time, remove the lamb from the oven and carefully spoon half of the miso harissa over the fat side of the lamb, spreading it evenly with the back of the spoon. Put it back in the oven, miso side up, for 3 more minutes.

Remove the lamb from the oven and let it rest for 10 minutes before slicing into separate chops.

Preheat the grill/broiler to 200°C (400°F) or to medium-high.

Put each lamb chop (cut side up) on a baking sheet lined with baking parchment. Spread a teaspoonful of the miso harissa on the surface of each lamb chop, then grill/broil the lamb for 3–4 minutes until the miso caramelizes on top but the lamb is still pink and tender inside. Serve straight away, garnished with watercress and pomegranate seeds.

KAMO NO NIGIRI

The culinary bond between France and Japan is undeniable. This dish is a little reverence to both countries' shared appreciation for each other's cuisine: the famous French Canard à l'Orange 'à la Japonaise'. For this, I cook the duck tataki-style and turn it into nigiri with a dollop of savoury miso-marmalade on top. It looks spectacular, tastes heavenly and oozes decadence.

2 duck breasts (340 g/12 oz. combined weight), skin scored in diagonal lines to help the fat render
360 g/12½ oz. Cooked Seasoned Sushi Rice (see pages 30–31)
finely grated zest of ½ orange

NEGI MARMALADE MISO SAUCE
2 tbsp barley miso (or red miso)
2 tbsp mirin
80 g/2¾ oz. leek, white part only, very finely chopped
2 tbsp no-added-sugar marmalade

MAKES 24

Heat a dry frying pan/skillet over medium–high heat. Place the duck breasts in the hot pan, skin-side down, and leave them to fry for 5 minutes until the skin is golden and crispy. Use folded kitchen paper to mop up any excess fat that has come out of the skin into the pan.

Flip the duck breasts over and fry for a further 5–8 minutes. Use tongs to turn the duck breasts on their sides to make sure they are evenly cooked all the way around. The centre of the duck breasts will remain pink, but you can cook them for longer if you prefer. Remove the duck from the pan and set aside to rest for 5–10 minutes.

Meanwhile, make the negi marmalade miso sauce. Add the miso and mirin to a small saucepan over low heat and stir. Add the chopped leek, then simmer for 1–2 minutes. Add the marmalade and stir well to combine. Remove the pan from the heat and set aside.

Wipe off any excess juice that has come out of the duck breasts, then carve them into thin slices.

Moisten your hands with a little water (try to remember to do this every time just before you touch the rice). Take a tablespoon of sushi rice and gently shape it into an oval. Repeat with the remaining rice to make about 24 ovals.

Take a piece of duck and place the best looking side face-down (as this will end up being on top). Place a rice ball on top of the duck and use your thumb to make an indentation in the centre of the rice. Turn the rice and duck, duck-side up, then use the other hand to shape the rice underneath into an even oblong by pushing gently from the sides with your thumb and forefinger. Press the top to flatten it with your forefinger and middle finger and stick the duck and rice together. The duck should cover the rice. Repeat for the remaining rice balls and sliced duck.

Top each nigiri with a pea-sized dot of negi marmalade miso sauce and garnish with a little orange zest just before serving.

LAMB NO GYOZA

Gyoza may originate from China but, much like ramen, they are now a well-loved part of Japanese food culture: you'll find them on the menus of ramen bars, izakayas or chuka (Japanese-style Chinese) restaurants. They now even have their own dedicated speciality joints, which offer different takes on the pork classic. This gave me the idea to make them with lamb and add a touch of cumin for a little Middle Eastern warmth. It works wonderfully, and although gyoza are the perfect side dish to share with friends and family, you might want to take heed of a new trend in Japan: the Gyo-jo or Gyoza Joshi (Gyoza Girls), real potsticker aficionados who go out to eat their gyoza alongside a glass of very cold beer!

100 g/3½ oz. Chinese cabbage, finely chopped
½ tsp salt
125 g/4½ oz. minced/ground lamb (20% fat)
1 tsp finely grated garlic
1 tsp peeled and finely grated fresh ginger
25 g/¾ oz. red onion, finely chopped
½ tbsp sake
½ tbsp mirin
½ tbsp sesame oil
1 tsp soy sauce
1 tbsp red miso
pinch of black pepper
pinch of ground cumin
20 store-bought gyoza wrappers
½ tbsp vegetable oil, for frying
½ tbsp toasted sesame oil, for frying

SPICY DIPPING SAUCE
2 tbsp soy sauce
2 tbsp rice vinegar
2 tbsp mirin
1 tsp chilli oil

26–28-cm/10¼–11-inch frying pan/skillet with a lid

MAKES 20 DUMPLINGS

Put the chopped cabbage in a bowl, add the salt and mix well. Leave for 10 minutes to draw out the excess water.

Meanwhile, to make the spicy dipping sauce mix all the ingredients together in a small bowl. Set aside.

To make the gyoza filling, mix the lamb with your hands until smooth, then add the garlic, ginger, red onion, sake, mirin, sesame oil, soy sauce, red miso, black pepper and ground cumin. Rinse the cabbage in a colander, then squeeze it to extract as much liquid as possible. Add the cabbage to the lamb mixture and mix everything together until evenly combined.

Prepare a small bowl of water. To construct the gyoza, put 1 teaspoon of filling in the middle of a gyoza wrapper. Wet the edges of the wrapper with a dab of water. Fold the wrapper in half over the filling and make seven pleats where the edges connect, squeezing them together to ensure the filling is well sealed inside. Repeat the process for the remaining wrappers and filling.

When you are ready to cook the gyoza, heat a large frying pan/skillet over high heat, then add the vegetable oil and toasted sesame oil. Working quickly, put all the gyoza into the pan. Let them sizzle for about 2 minutes until the bottoms of the gyoza start to turn brown.

Pour 100 ml/⅓ cup water into the pan from the rim, then quickly cover the pan with the lid so that not too much steam is lost. Reduce the heat to medium and steam the gyoza for 4 minutes. The water will evaporate as the gyoza steam, leaving the bottoms crispy.

Remove the gyoza from the pan and serve immediately with the spicy dipping sauce while they are still crispy.

Pictured on pages 84–85

TORI NO SUI GYOZA

Sui Gyoza are softer and squishier than their potsticker sibling. Here, the delicious chicken dumplings are boiled instead of fried with oil, making them a healthier and lighter option.

100 g/3½ oz. Chinese cabbage, finely chopped

½ tsp salt

125 g/4½ oz. skinless, boneless chicken thighs

25 g/¾ oz. fresh coriander/cilantro, leaves only, roughly chopped

½ tsp peeled and finely grated fresh ginger

grated zest of ¼ lime

1 tbsp sake

1 tbsp mirin

1 tbsp sesame oil

1½ tbsp soy sauce

¼ tsp sansho pepper (optional)

20 store-bought gyoza wrappers

DIPPING SAUCE

2 tbsp soy sauce

2 tbsp rice vinegar

2 tbsp mirin

1 tsp chilli oil

½ tbsp toasted white sesame seeds

1 tsp peeled and finely chopped fresh ginger (optional)

MAKES 20 DUMPLINGS

Put the chopped cabbage in a bowl, add the salt and mix well. Leave for 10 minutes to draw out the excess water.

Meanwhile, to make the dipping sauce, mix all the ingredients together in a small bowl. Set aside.

Rinse the cabbage in a colander, then squeeze it to extract as much water as possible.

Mince the chicken thighs until smooth in a food processor, then add the cabbage, coriander/cilantro leaves, grated ginger, lime zest, sake, mirin, sesame oil, soy sauce and sansho pepper (if using). Pulse briefly in the food processor until the ingredients are well combined, then set aside.

Prepare a small bowl of water. To construct the gyoza, put 1 teaspoon of chicken filling in the middle of a gyoza wrapper. Wet the edges of the wrapper with a dab of water. Fold the wrapper in half over the filling and squeeze the edges together to ensure the filling is well sealed inside. Repeat the process for the remaining wrappers and filling.

When you are ready to cook the gyoza, bring a large saucepan of water to the boil. Add 7–10 gyoza at a time to the boiling water and cook for about 6–7 minutes over medium-high heat. When the gyoza are cooked, they will float to the surface of the water.

Remove from the pan using a slotted spoon and set aside briefly while you cook the remaining gyoza. Serve immediately with the dipping sauce.

Pictured on pages 84–85

YUZU SHIO RAMEN

You must all know what ramen is by now... the famous noodle soup that is comforting, vibrant and eaten very hot in a few slurps! Did you know that there are four kinds of ramen: shoyu, miso, tonkotsu and shio? This is shio ramen, which is seasoned primarily with salt or shio, giving the broth a complex umami flavour.

CHICKEN STOCK/BROTH SOUP

2 kg/4 lb. 6 oz. chicken carcasses

20 g/¾ oz. fresh ginger, peeled and thinly sliced

2 spring onions/scallions, torn in half

400 ml/1⅔ cups Kombu & Katsuobushi Dashi (see page 33)

2 tbsp sake

1 tbsp fine sea salt

1 tbsp golden caster/granulated sugar

1 tbsp yuzu juice

POACHED CHICKEN BREASTS

2 skin-on boneless chicken breasts

¼ tsp salt

2 spring onions/scallions, cut in half

1 tsp peeled and thinly sliced fresh ginger

75 ml/⅓ cup sake

2–3 lemons (to taste), zest peeled with a vegetable peeler

TO SERVE

2 UK large/US extra-large eggs

4 portions of dried ramen noodles

2 spring onions/scallions, thinly sliced

1 tbsp white sesame seeds

SERVES 4

For the chicken stock/broth, add the chicken carcasses, ginger and spring onions/scallions to a very large saucepan. Cover with cold water, then bring to the boil. Reduce the heat to low and simmer, uncovered, for at least 2 hours. Skim any scum off the surface and top up with water as needed.

Strain the stock/broth and set aside (discarding the vegetables and carcasses). It should make about 1.6 litres/quarts.

To make the broth into soup, heat the chicken stock/broth in a medium saucepan over medium heat until gently simmering. Add the katsuobushi dashi, sake, salt and sugar. Simmer until the sugar and salt have dissolved. Remove from the heat and add the yuzu juice. Set aside.

For the poached chicken breasts, season the chicken with the salt. Add the chicken to a separate medium saucepan with the spring onions/scallions, ginger, sake and 150 ml/⅔ cup water. Cover the pan with a lid and bring to the boil, then reduce the heat to low and simmer for 15 minutes.

Make sure your chicken is cooked by poking a skewer into the thickest part. If the liquid coming out of the hole is clear, then it should be cooked. If it's still slightly pink, cook for 5 more minutes over medium-low heat.

Turn the heat off, then add the lemon zest. Leave the chicken in the saucepan with the lid on for 5–10 minutes, this will ensure it is moist and well-seasoned with the broth. (Note: you can keep the cooked chicken in the cooking liquid in an airtight container for up to 3 days in the fridge.)

Bring 1.5 litres/quarts water to the boil in a medium saucepan. Carefully add the eggs and boil for exactly 7 minutes over medium-high heat for soft egg yolks. Immediately transfer the eggs to a bowl and place under cold running water until cool. Peel the eggs and set aside.

Reheat the soup over low heat until hot. Meanwhile, cook the ramen noodles by following the packet instructions until al dente, then drain well. Thinly slice the poached chicken and cut the cooked eggs in half.

To serve, divide the hot soup between serving bowls and add the cooked noodles. Top with the thinly sliced chicken breast, the halved boiled eggs, sliced spring onions/scallions and sesame seeds.

魚と魚介
FISH &
SEAFOOD

EBI TO AVOCADO NO WASABI MAYO AE

海老とアボカドの
わさびマヨ和え
*KING PRAWN/SHRIMP &
AVOCADO DRESSED WITH
WASABI MAYONNAISE*

A prawn/shrimp cocktail is probably one of the most recognized seafood appetizers in both the UK and US. The classic version is dressed with Marie Rose sauce (made from mayonnaise and tomato ketchup), with a hint of Tabasco. Here is my twist on the classic, with a gorgeous wasabi mayo to offset the sweetness of the delicate seafood.

1 ripe avocado
freshly squeezed juice of ½ lime
180 g/6½ oz. raw king prawns/
   jumbo shrimp, peeled
Wasabi Mayo (see page 41)

SERVES 4

Peel, stone/pit and dice the avocado. Sprinkle the diced avocado flesh with the lime juice to stop it from browning and set aside.

To devein the prawns/shrimp without damaging them, insert a skewer at the tail near the back end where you can see the black vein. Carefully pull out the black vein from the hole you have made with the skewer. Devein all the prawns/shrimp.

Bring a large saucepan of water to the boil and prepare a large bowl of cold water. Add the prawns/shrimp to the pan and cook for 2 minutes until the flesh turns white and orange.

Remove the prawns/shrimp from the pan using a slotted spoon and immediately transfer them to the bowl of cold water to stop the cooking process. When the prawns/shrimp have cooled (after about 5 minutes), remove them from the water and pat dry with kitchen paper.

Divide the diced avocado between the bottom of four serving glasses. Spoon some wasabi mayo on top, followed by the prawns/shrimp. Garnish the prawns/shrimp with dill fronds and serve. Dessert forks are helpful if serving at a cocktail party.

HAMACHI USUZUKURI

*YELLOWTAIL CARPACCIO WITH
ONION SOY DRESSING*

Of all the types of fish we eat in Japan, hamachi (yellowtail) is a favourite amongst home cooks and professional chefs alike. The confusing part might be that it's a fish with many names! Hamachi, buri, yellowtail, amberjack... it all comes down to the age and size of the fish as well as the Japanese region you're in. Don't panic though! If you ask your fishmonger for some hamachi or yellowtail, he'll know what you're after. Prepared carpaccio-style, hamachi has a semi-soft texture and its flavours are delicate, rich and slightly sweet. It pairs beautifully with citrus as you'll see with this recipe with the onion soy dressing.

300 g/10½ oz. sashimi-grade hamachi saku (yellowtail)
4 handfuls of mixed salad leaves
Onion Soy Dressing (see page 35)
1 tbsp olive oil
pinch of fresh herbs, such as baby shiso leaves or oregano flowers
1 tbsp store-bought crispy fried shallots

SERVES 4

For slicing the fish, we use a technique called usu-zukuri. Lay the hamachi saku on a clean chopping board horizontally in front of you, with thickest side away from you. Insert the heel of your sashimi knife (yanagiba) or a carving knife into the fish about 8 mm/⅓ inch from the left side of the fish (if you are left-handed, slice from the right side instead), holding the fish steady with your other fingers, pull the knife gently towards you in one stroke. Relax and try not to force the knife through quickly. Using gentle movements with just a little pressure is key to not damaging the fish. Wipe and clean the surface of the chopping board with a damp clean cloth if it gets slippery along the way. Keep slicing the rest of the fillet until you have 12 slices. Chill in the fridge until you are ready to serve.

To serve, divide the mixed leaf salad between serving plates. Roll up the hamachi slices and place them on the serving plates next to the salad.

Drizzle over the onion soy dressing just before you serve, then drizzle drops of olive oil on top. Lastly, sprinkle over the herbs and crispy fried shallots. Serve straight away.

HITOKUCHI TEMAKI SUSHI

Temaki sushi are literally ' hand' (te) 'rolled' (maki) sushi and are the easiest sushi to make. In Japan, it's very common to throw temaki party amongst family and friends. It's a fun, casual affair: everyone gathers around a table filled with colourful prepped ingredients and the party unfolds as temaki are made, chats are had and drinks are drunk... For this recipe, I cut the nori in half to make shorter rolls. They become small-bite sushi (hitokuchi), which are easier to eat! It also gives you the opportunity to try even more flavour combinations.

10 nori sheets, each cut
    into four equal squares
1.2 kg/2 lb. 10 oz. Seasoned
    Sushi Rice (see pages
    30–31)

FILLINGS
4 okra
80 g/2¾ oz. salmon roe
750 g/1 lb. 10 oz. selection
    of sashimi-quality fish
    (such as salmon, otoro/
    fatty tuna, akami tuna and
    hamachi/yellowtail), cut
    into 7-cm/2¾-inch x
    1-cm/⅜-inch sticks
    (see opposite)
4 cooked king prawns/jumbo
    shrimp, peeled and
    deveined (buy ready-
    cooked or see page 90
    for how to cook)
1 ripe avocado, peeled,
    stoned/pitted and sliced
    lengthwise, sprinkled with
    1 tsp freshly squeezed
    lemon juice to stop it from
    browning
7-cm/2¾-inch piece of
    cucumber, seeds removed
    and cut into fine sticks

NEGI TORO
50 g/1¾ oz. otoro
    (fatty tuna) trimmings,
    finely minced
50 g/1¾ oz. akami tuna
    trimmings, finely minced
1 spring onion/scallion,
    thinly sliced
wasabi, to taste (optional)

TO SERVE
8 fresh shiso leaves
    (or substitute with other
    herbs such as chives,
    dill or mint)
8 fresh coriander/cilantro
    leaves
10-cm/4-inch piece of
    daikon radish, peeled
    and thinly sliced
80 g/2¾ oz. pickled ginger
soy sauce

**MAKES 40 BITES
(SERVES 4)**

Soak the sliced spring onion/scallion and daikon radish in cold water for 10 minutes. Drain well.

Blanch the okra in a large saucepan of salted boiling water for 2 minutes. Drain in a colander, then rinse under cold running water to stop the cooking process. Cut the okra in half lengthways, then place in a serving dish with the salmon roe.

For the negi toro, mix the minced tuna trimmings with the spring onion/scallion and place in a serving dish alongside all the other ingredients on their own separate serving dishes.

To assemble the sushi, hold a square of nori flat on your hand, shiny side down. Take a bite-sized piece of sushi rice and gently spread it over the centre of the nori.

Spread a little wasabi along the centre of the rice, if you like, then top the rice with your favourite fillings.

Fold the nori in half over the filling and eat immediately while the nori is still perfectly crisp. If not eaten immediately, the nori will begin to get soggy. Enjoy this sushi with as many varieties of fillings as you like!

Pictured on pages 94–95

HOW TO CUT SALMON SASHIMI

Make sure to buy the fish on the day you are preparing your dish, or within 24 hours of serving it. Another option is to buy frozen fish for sushi and sashimi. It needs to be consumed within 24 hours of defrosting.

To cut salmon for temaki (see below left), place the fish on a clean chopping board with the streaks running horizontally. Gently hold the fish with your fingers while inserting the top part of the knife across the grain of the fish. Draw the knife as gently as possible towards you, across the white streaks of the flesh.

To cut salmon for Aburi Sushi (see page 101) or Temari Sushi (see page 98), place the fish on a clean chopping board horizontally (see below right). Gently hold the fish with your fingers and insert your blade starting with the heel of your knife. Position it diagonally at the edge of the fish (left side for right-handed) and move the knife as gently as possible towards you across the white streaks in the flesh. One slice of fish should be 3 x 7 cm/1¼ x 2¾ inches wide and 4 mm/⅛ inch thick.

It is best to use a long, skinny, sharp knife or a specialized 'yanagiba' knife for slicing sashimi. The blade lengths of these specialized knives vary, but the most suitable length for the below technique is 24–27 cm/9½–10½ inches.

TEMARI SUSHI

手毬寿司

BALL-SHAPED SUSHI

These are bite-sized sushi, with 'hito' referring to 'bite' and 'kuchi' to 'mouth'. In Kyoto's Gion quarter, where you can spot geishas and maikos, you'll find plenty of sushi joints where these traditional entertainers can eat without ruining their fabulous make-up. Your guests probably won't come as done up as geishas but they can't not be impressed by this spectacular selection of sushi!

PRAWN/SHRIMP

150 g/5¼ oz. Cooked Seasoned
   Sushi Rice (see pages 30–31)
10 steamed king prawns/jumbo
   shrimp
30 g/1 oz. salmon roe

MAKES 10 TEMARI

AKAMI (TUNA) ZUKE

150 g/5¼ oz. Cooked Seasoned
   Sushi Rice (see pages 30–31)
150 g/5¼ oz. sashimi-grade akami
   (lean tuna), sliced (see page 97)
Banno Sauce (see page 35) or
   soy sauce
1 tsp grated bottarga (salted cured
   fish roe)

MAKES 10 TEMARI

Akami tuna can be cured and seasoned in a curing process called zuke. Submerge the slices of akami in the banno sauce for 10 minutes. Drain well and set aside.

SALMON

150 g/5¼ oz. Cooked Seasoned
   Sushi Rice (see pages 30–31)
150 g/5¼ oz. sashimi-grade
   salmon, sliced (see page 97)

MAKES 10 TEMARI

KOMBU CURED SEA BASS

1 tbsp sake, mixed with 1 tbsp water
2 kombu sheets, 9 x 20 cm/3½ x
   8 inches
1 fillet of sashimi-grade sea bass,
   skinned and pin-boned, sliced
   (see page 97)

MAKES 10 TEMARI

To cure the sea bass, sprinkle the sake water over the two sheets of kombu on both sides and set them aside for 10 minutes until reconstituted.

Place the sea bass slices evenly in one layer between the two sheets of kombu, so that all the surfaces of the fish come into contact with the kombu. Wrap it tightly in clingfilm/plastic wrap and refrigerate for at least 30 minutes and up to 2 hours. Remove the fish from the kombu and it is ready to top your sushi.

TO SERVE
fresh herbs, such as sansho,
   shiso and nasturtium leaves
lemon slices, cut into triangles
wasabi
soy sauce

HOW TO SHAPE TEMARI SUSHI
Take a tablespoonful (15 g/½ oz.) of sushi rice and shape it into a small ball.

Put a 30-cm/12-inch square of clingfilm/plastic wrap on a flat work surface. Put a slice of fish or prawn/jumbo shrimp in the centre of the clingfilm/plastic wrap and a sushi rice ball on top. Gather the clingfilm/plastic wrap up around the rice, then twist to compress the rice and toppings together.

Unwrap the rice ball and place it on a plate. Repeat for the remaining rice balls and toppings of your choice.

Garnish with fresh herbs and lemon slices cut into triangles. Serve with wasabi and soy sauce.

Recipe continued overleaf »

Both recipes pictured on page 99

RAINBOW CHARD MAKI

5-cm/2-inch piece of carrot, peeled,
thinly sliced and cut out using a maple
leaf cutter
2 red radishes, thinly sliced
2 rainbow chard leaves
150 g/5¼ oz. Cooked Seasoned Sushi
Rice (see pages 30–31)
20 g/¾ oz. pickled ginger, finely
chopped
1 tbsp sesame seeds

bamboo sushi rolling mat

MAKES 12 BITES

Put the carrot slices and red radishes to soak in cold water until needed.

Blanch the rainbow chard leaves for 1 minute in a large saucepan of salted boiling water. Immediately drain in a colander and rinse under cold running water. Drain again and pat dry with kitchen paper. Remove and discard the stems. Set aside.

Mix the rice with the ginger and sesame seeds.

Place the bamboo mat in front of you, with the bamboo running horizontally. Place one chard leaf horizontally at the front of the mat. Lightly wet your hands, then take half of the rice (75 g/2¾ oz.) and shape it into a cylinder, on top of the chard. Lift the edge of the mat closest to you and cover the rice with the mat. Press along the mat with your hands to mould the shape into a cylinder. Continue rolling the mat away from you until fully rolled. Press into the sides and top of the mat to create a cuboid. Unroll the mat to leave you with a cuboid sushi roll.

Wipe a large knife with a wet towel and cut the roll in half widthways. Place the two halves side by side and cut each one into three pieces, making six portions in total. Repeat the process with the remaining rice and rainbow chard.

HITOKUCHI INARI

3 abura-age (fried tofu pouches)
1½ tbsp sake
1 tbsp light brown soft sugar
1 tbsp mirin
1½ tbsp soy sauce
1 cinnamon stick
peel from 1 orange
360 g/12½ oz. Cooked Seasoned Sushi
Rice (see pages 30–31)
2 tsp white sesame seeds
30 g/1 oz. pickled ginger, finely chopped

MAKES 12 PIECES

Wash the abura-age (fried tofu pouches) in a bowl of hot water to remove the excess oil on the surface. Drain, pat dry and leave until they are cool. Cut the abura-age into quarters and set aside.

Put the sake, brown sugar, mirin, soy sauce, cinnamon stick and orange peel in a saucepan with 100 ml/⅓ cup water and bring to the boil.

Add the abura-age to the pan and bring back to the boil. Reduce the heat to low, then cover the pan with a lid and simmer for 15 minutes, turning the abura-age over halfway through. Remove the pan from the heat and leave the tofu to cool down in the liquid.

Meanwhile, gently mix the sushi rice with the sesame seeds and ginger. Wet your hands slightly to stop the rice from sticking, then divide the rice into 12 equal 20-g/¾-oz. portions and roll into balls.

Remove the tofu pouches from the cooking liquid and gently squeeze out the excess liquid.

Stuff a rice ball into each small triangular tofu pouch. Try to push the rice right into the corners of the pouch. Wrap the overhanging edges of the tofu pouch around the rice to seal it inside. Serve with the join underneath, pointy side up.

ABURI SUSHI

Salmon nigiri is probably one of the best-loved types of sushi, with legions of fans around the world, but have you tried it aburi-style? Literally meaning 'flame seared', this method involves using a blow torch to gently scorch the surface of the fish, transforming its flavour and texture. When the buttery and silky texture of the salmon is combined with the crispy, charred, smoky essence of the grilled fish, you can close your eyes and think you're in heaven! It's such a quick, easy touch to add to your nigiri, which will earn you performance kudos from your guests!

360 g/12½ oz. sashimi-grade
   salmon belly, skinned
sansho pepper, to serve

SUSHI RICE
180 g/6½ oz. sushi rice
   (Japanese short-grain rice)
2 tbsp rice vinegar
1 tbsp golden caster/granulated
   sugar
½ tsp salt

NIKIRI SAUCE
60 ml/¼ cup soy sauce
60 ml/¼ cup mirin
2 tbsp sake

cook's blow torch

MAKES 24

To cook the sushi rice, place the rice in a sieve/strainer and rinse under cold running water until the water becomes clear. Leave to drain in the sieve/strainer for 30 minutes.

Place the rice in a small saucepan with 200 ml/generous ¾ cup water. Cover the pan with a lid (don't remove the lid until the rice has rested). Bring to the boil over high heat. When the rice starts to boil, turn the heat down and simmer for 9 minutes. When the cooking time is up, remove the pan from the heat, leave the lid on and rest for 10 minutes.

Meanwhile, mix the rice vinegar, golden caster sugar and salt together in a separate bowl.

Wet the surface of a mixing bowl and spatula to prevent the rice sticking. Turn the rice out into the bowl. Pour the vinegar mixture over the rice and gently use the spatula to mix the rice. Cover with a damp cloth and leave to cool at room temperature.

To make the nikiri sauce, mix the soy sauce, mirin and sake together in a small saucepan. Warm through over low heat for 5 minutes. Set aside.

Cut the salmon belly into slices on the diagonal across the white streaks in the flesh (see page 97). One slice of salmon should be about 3 x 7 cm/ 1¼ x 2¾ inches and 4 mm/⅛-¼ inch thick so it will cover the rice underneath. Keep the sliced salmon in the fridge until needed.

To shape your nigiri, wet one hand with water, then rub it together with the other hand so that your hands are moist but not dripping wet. This helps stop the rice from sticking to your hands while you shape the nigiri. Try to remember to do it every time just before you touch the rice. Take a tablespoon of sushi rice and gently shape it in your hands to make a small oval ball. Repeat with the remaining rice to make about 24 balls.

Pictured on page 103

Recipe continued overleaf >>

Take a slice of salmon belly and place the best looking side of it face-down (as this will end up being on top). Place a rice ball on top of the salmon and use your thumb to make an indentation in the centre, this will make for a lighter textured rice. Turn the rice and salmon, salmon-side up, then use the other hand to shape the rice underneath into an even oblong by pushing gently from the sides with your thumb and forefinger. Press the top to flatten it with your forefinger and middle finger and stick the salmon and rice together. The salmon should cover the rice. Repeat for the remaining rice balls and sliced salmon.

Brush each piece of salmon twice with some nikiri sauce.

It's best to eat aburi right after it's seared, so line up 2–4 nigiri pieces together (depending on how many people are ready to eat them right away) as close as possible to protect the sides of the rice from burning, then quickly sear the salmon with a blow torch for 3 seconds. This will char the surface of the salmon and create a smoky flavour without completely cooking it.

Sprinkle the nigiri with sansho pepper and serve straight away. Repeat the blow-torching process for the remaining aburi as needed.

For the best eating experience, pinch the aburi to hold it together with your fingers and turn it upside down so you can taste the best part of the fish first on your tongue. Eat it all in one go for maximum enjoyment.

NOTE *The aburi cooking method works particularly well with any fatty, oily fish such as raw fatty tuna belly, pickled mackerel and marbled Wagyu meat. It also goes well with shellfish, such as scallops and prawns/shrimp, etc. Really, it works with anything you fancy adding an extra chargrilled flavour and texture to.*

If you are making this salmon recipe, you may need to purchase a centre part of a whole fillet, which includes the belly, back and centre part where the spine is. Both the belly and back part of the fillet can be divided and used for sashimi and sushi. However, I recommend that you don't use the centre part where the spine is, as it has more sinew and is hard to eat raw.

SAKE NO MISO MAPLE YAKI

鮭の味噌メープル焼き

MISO & MAPLE MARINATED SALMON

It is time to dethrone the usual salmon teriyaki everyone expects of Japanese cuisine, and surprise your guests with your new go-to salmon recipe! The soft flesh of the salmon works wonderfully with this sweet miso marinade and the hints of orange zest really add fragrance to this hassle-free recipe. Combined with little florets of pickled cauliflower, it's a canapé your friends won't forget!

500 g/1 lb. 2 oz. skin-on salmon fillet, scaled and pin-boned
½ tsp fine sea salt
1 tbsp toasted white sesame seeds, to garnish
a bunch of fresh chives

ORANGE MISO MARINADE
90 g/3 oz. sweet white miso (saikyo miso)
2 tbsp mirin
2 tbsp maple syrup
2 tsp finely grated orange zest, plus extra for garnishing
1 tsp peeled and finely grated fresh ginger

PICKLED CAULIFLOWER
1 cauliflower
120 ml/½ cup rice vinegar
4 tbsp caster/granulated sugar
2 tsp salt
1 dried chilli (optional)

baking sheet lined with baking parchment
bamboo skewers

MAKES 20 BITES

Dice the salmon into 3-cm/1¼-inch square cubes, then sprinkle it with the salt and set aside for 20 minutes. Wipe off any excess moisture from the fish with kitchen paper.

To make the orange miso marinade, combine the sweet white miso, mirin, maple syrup, orange zest and ginger in a bowl.

Place the diced salmon in a container with a lid, pour over the marinade and gently stir together. Seal the container and leave to marinate for at least 30 minutes or up to 24 hours in the fridge.

To pickle the cauliflower, bring a medium saucepan of water to the boil. Meanwhile, cut the cauliflower into 20 equal, small bite-sized florets. Add the cauliflower pieces to the pan and boil for 2 minutes. Drain well, then put the cauliflower florets into a container with an airtight lid or in a resealable bag.

Mix the rice vinegar, sugar, salt and chilli (if using) together with 120 ml/ ½ cup water in a jug/pitcher, then pour the pickling liquid over the top of the cauliflower. If you are using a container, shake the container to make sure each piece of cauliflower is coated in pickling liquid. Or, if you are using a resealable bag, dip the bag in a bowl of cold water to remove any air and seal immediately so it is almost vacuum-packed. Leave to marinate for a minimum of 30 minutes or up to 24 hours in the fridge.

When you are nearly ready to serve, preheat the oven to 220°C /200°C fan (425°F) Gas 7.

Gently wipe most of the miso off the salmon with a butter knife or palette knife. Place the salmon, skin-side up, on the lined baking sheet and bake in the preheated oven for about 7 minutes (depending on the thickness of salmon) until cooked and slightly browned.

To serve, skewer a piece of cauliflower, then a piece of salmon from the skin side. Sprinkle over orange zest and toasted sesame seeds to garnish. Place the skewers on a bed of fresh chives to serve.

SUZUKI NO KOBUJIME

CURED SEA BASS WITH LIME PONZU SAUCE & TRUFFLE OIL

The ancient kobujime method of curing fish between sheets of kombu comes from the Toyama prefecture where 'the king of seaweed' has always enjoyed a high status in the regional cuisine. This preservation technique works particularly well with sea bass or sea bream, as they are both delicate white meat fish that take on a wonderfully firm texture when cured. To prepare this dish, the fish is tightly wrapped in between two layers of kombu. The kombu tightens up the surface of the fish, giving it a firmer texture and infusing it with its umami, boosting the fish with sweetness and depth of flavour. Serve with refreshing lime ponzu sauce and a dash of white truffle oil. An elegant yet simple dish to impress your friends!

2–3 tbsp sake
4 kombu sheets, 9 x 20 cm/
   3½ x 8 inches
2 sashimi-grade sea bass fillets,
   skinned and pin-boned

LIME PONZU SAUCE
2 tbsp freshly squeezed lime juice
2 tbsp soy sauce
1½ tbsp mirin

TO SERVE
½ tsp white truffle oil
handful of fresh coriander/cilantro
   leaves
2 red radishes, thinly sliced, soaked
   in cold water until needed

SERVES 4

To cure the sea bass, first sprinkle a little sake over each kombu sheet. Leave for 10 minutes until slightly reconstituted.

Next, place each sea bass fillet between two sheets of kombu. Wrap each sea bass fillet and kombu tightly in clingfilm/plastic wrap and refrigerate for a minimum of 2 hours or up to 24 hours.

Meanwhile, mix the ingredients for the lime ponzu sauce together in a small bowl and set aside.

When the sea bass is ready, unwrap it and discard the clingfilm/plastic wrap and kombu. (Do not be concerned if the kombu is now sticky and slimy after curing the fish, this is absolutely normal.) Place a fillet of fish horizontally in front of you on a chopping board, would-be skin side down, then cut it into slices diagonally from the head to the tail, to give slices with a wide surface area.

Quick-curing option: It is possible to lightly cure the sea bass in as little as 30 minutes if you are short on time. Simply thinly slice the sea bass diagonally first (see method above), then place the pieces between two sheets of sake-soaked kombu. Wrap tightly in clingfilm/plastic wrap and refrigerate for a minimum of 30 minutes and up to 2 hours.

Just before serving, place the cured fish on a large serving plate and pour over the lime ponzu sauce. Drizzle over the white truffle oil and scatter with coriander/cilantro leaves and sliced red radishes. Serve immediately.

NOTE *Really do serve immediately! Don't leave the fish in the ponzu sauce for too long before serving as it will further cure. You can also serve the lime ponzu sauce separately for dipping the fish if you prefer.*

NAMA GAKI

In Japan, we LOVE oysters; we eat them raw, deep-fried, in broths, in stews... you name it, we love them! They're also very easy to find in supermarkets in packs of 20, shucked out of their shells and in their juice – even here they remain a delicacy due to their hefty price tag. Here I am sharing my favourite oyster recipe which puts the raw oyster front and centre. I use rice vinegar for the dressing, which is much rounder than the usual wine vinegar or squeeze of lemon juice. I cut it with soy sauce and olive oil for a smooth and enticing finish.

6 oysters
3 tbsp fine salt mixed with 1 tbsp cold water
1 tsp extra virgin olive oil, for drizzling

DAIKON & SOY SAUCE DRESSING
1 tbsp soy sauce
1 tbsp rice vinegar
10-cm/4-inch piece of daikon (or 6 red radishes)
1 tbsp very thinly sliced spring onion/scallion

oyster knife

MAKES 6

To make the daikon and soy sauce dressing, mix the soy sauce and rice vinegar together in a glass jar. Peel the skin off the daikon and finely grate it. Squeeze the grated daikon gently to remove the excess water. Mix the grated daikon and sliced spring onion/scallion together in a small bowl. Set aside (you will combine these just before serving).

To open/shuck the oysters, place an oyster flat-side up on a damp cloth to stop it slipping while you open it. Hold the oyster steady with another damp cloth to protect your hand, then use the other hand to insert the tip of an oyster knife into the hinge at the corner of the pointy side. Gently push and wiggle the tip of the knife deeper into the hinge (about 1.5 cm/½ inch in), then twist the knife 90 degrees to open the oyster. (Note: If your knife is not inserted deep enough into the hinge, the end of the knife could break/chip when you twist it. If you aren't sure whether your knife is inserted far enough, try to cover the oyster with the cloth when you twist the knife.)

Separate the oyster from the top shell (flat side) first using the oyster knife, then separate the bottom of the oyster from the shell. Repeat for the remaining oysters.

Put the wet salt on the large plate (this will hold the oysters steady) and add the oysters. Place a little grated daikon and spring onion/scallion on top of each oyster.

Pour the soy-vinegar mixture over the grated daikon on each oyster so that it absorbs the sauce, then drizzle over the extra virgin olive oil and eat immediately.

IKA SHUMAI

Shumai are the steamed dumpling favourites at dim sum restaurants. They are traditionally Chinese, but this particular version is definitely Japanese and actually comes from my hometown, Yobuko in Kyushu. This town is known for its fish market and particularly for the translucent squid or ika you can get there. Ika Shumai are steamed squid and white fish dumplings, which are beautifully wrapped in thin strips of gyoza wrappers to emulate a blooming flower. The squid gives a natural sweetness to the dumplings, while the strips of gyoza wrapper add an airy, fluffy texture to your mouthful.

10 gyoza wrappers
6 large lettuce leaves
English mustard, to serve

FILLING
200 g/7 oz. cod, skinned
   and roughly diced
120 g/4½ oz. fresh squid,
   roughly chopped
1 egg white
1 shallot, finely chopped
½ tsp peeled and finely grated
   fresh ginger
¼ tsp fine salt
1 tsp golden caster/granulated sugar
1 tbsp sake
1 tbsp toasted sesame oil
2 tsp fish sauce
3 tbsp katakuriko (potato starch)

SU JOYU DIPPING SAUCE
2 tbsp rice vinegar
2 tbsp mirin
2 tbsp soy sauce

20-cm/8-inch steamer

MAKES 12

To make the su joyu dipping sauce, combine all the ingredients in a small bowl and set aside.

For the dumpling filling, put the cod and half of the squid in a food processor. Pulse to make a paste. Add the egg white and pulse again to combine with the fish paste – this will help give it an airy texture.

Tip the fish mixture out into a mixing bowl, then add the remaining chopped squid, shallot, ginger, salt, sugar, sake, sesame oil, fish sauce and katakuriko. Mix until well combined, then chill the dumpling filling in the fridge for 30 minutes.

Meanwhile, make two separate piles with five gyoza wrappers each on a chopping board. Slice both piles of the gyoza wrappers into fine strips, as thin as matchsticks, then separate the layers so that they don't stick together. Place the gyoza strips in a sealed container until ready to use.

Bring a steamer to the boil.

Wet your hands a little to stop the fish mixture from sticking, then divide the mixture into twelve 35-g/1¼-oz. portions. Shape each one into a ball. Mix the gyoza strips to a give a messy texture (rather than having them all neatly positioned). Cover each fish ball with a nest of gyoza strips.

Use tongs or chopsticks to place three lettuce leaves at the bottom of the steamer to stop the dumplings from sticking to the surface. Place six dumplings into the steamer (spaced apart as they will swell up when cooking). Cover with a lid and steam over medium heat for 7 minutes.

Take the dumplings and the lettuce leaves out of the steamer, then repeat the cooking process with the remaining lettuce leaves and dumplings.

Serve the dumplings hot, with dots of English mustard on top and the su joyu dipping sauce.

HOTATE NO SHOYU BUTTER YAKI

ホタテの醤油バター焼き
GRILLED SCALLOPS WITH SOY BUTTER

When I was a little girl, every so often we would go to the yakitori-ya for a family meal. My favourite part was the end when my parents ordered the last dish, the king of the dishes: fresh grilled hotate! How excited I was! Cooking scallops open in their shells works wonderfully. The shell acts as a small dish and brings out a beautiful seafood aroma.

6 hand-dived scallops in shells
2 tbsp sake
60 g/½ stick unsalted butter, diced
2 tbsp soy sauce
shichimi spice mix

oyster knife

SERVES 6

You can either ask your fishmonger to prepare the scallops for you, or you can do it yourself. If preparing them yourself, check the shells – they should be tightly shut so you know the scallops are still alive.

Put the flat side of the shell down on a clean cloth on a chopping board (to stop it slipping). Insert an oyster knife between the two shells and gently twist to open the scallop. Carefully run a small paring knife along the inside of the bottom shell to separate the scallop from the shell. The shell should now open fully, so use a spoon to scoop the whole scallop onto the chopping board. Discard the flat shell but save the bowl-shaped shell. Carefully pull off the outer skirt by hand. You will now be left with the nice round scallop muscle and orange/white roe.

Rinse the scallop in a bowl of salted cold water (3% salt), then quickly pat it dry with kitchen paper. Repeat for the remaining scallops.

Place the scallops on a chopping board and dice each one into 2–4 pieces, depending on the size. Separate the roe from the muscle so it is easy to eat with chopsticks. Rinse out the bowl-shaped shells ready to use them for cooking the scallops.

Place one diced scallop back in each shell, then place a shell directly on the smallest hob/stove-top ring. Sprinkle over 1 tsp sake, then turn the heat to low and cook for about 3–4 minutes, turning the scallop pieces a few times, until they turn white and are evenly cooked. At the end of the cooking process, add 10 g/⅓ oz. diced butter to the top of the scallops and sprinkle with 1 tsp soy sauce. Turn the heat off while the butter is still melting. Sprinkle with shichimi spice mix, then use oven gloves to remove the hot shell from the stove and serve immediately.

Repeat for the remaining scallops.

NOTE *If you have more than one small hob/gas ring you can cook multiple scallops at one time. If you only have an induction or electric hob, the scallops can be cooked in a frying pan/skillet in the same way without shells. Just serve them in the shells for presentation.*

TAKOYAKI

FRIED ROUND DUMPLINGS
STUFFED WITH OCTOPUS

Along with okonomiyaki, takoyaki are probably one of the most famous Osakan street foods, but you can also find them everywhere across Japan. They are little round balls of batter, crispy on the outside, soft on the inside and stuffed with little nuggets of octopus. You'll need to buy a special pan (widely available online) to make takoyaki, but they're definitely worth it as they are such a perfect party food.

450 ml/scant 2 cups Dashi of your choice (see pages 32–33)

1 UK large/US extra-large egg

2 tsp light soy sauce

150 g/1 cup plus 2 tbsp plain/all-purpose flour, sifted

3½ tbsp vegetable oil, for frying

FILLING

200 g/7 oz. octopus tentacles

20 g/¾ oz. pickled ginger, finely chopped

2 spring onions/scallions, finely chopped

TO SERVE

120 g/4¼ oz. takoyaki sauce

60 g/2 oz. Japanese mayonnaise

10 g/⅓ oz. bonito flakes (katsuobushi)

2 tsp aonori seaweed flakes

iron takoyaki pan with 16 holes (each hole 4 cm/1½ inches wide)

MAKES 32

Whisk the dashi, egg and light soy sauce together in a large jug/pitcher. Sprinkle over the flour in two additions and gently whisk into the dashi mixture until incorporated into a smooth batter. Do not overmix.

Before you start cooking, make a simple but useful tool: scrunch some good-quality, thick kitchen paper tightly into a ball. Place the ball in the middle of another sheet of kitchen paper then wrap it around and twist the loose ends together to make a lollipop/candy on a stick shape.

Heat the takoyaki pan over high heat. When the pan is hot, dip the paper ball of the lollipop into the vegetable oil, then use it to oil each hole. Dip the paper in the oil again, then use it to coat the flat surface of the pan. You'll need to cover the whole surface of the pan in oil to avoid the batter sticking. There should be some oil pooling at the bottom of the holes.

Pour a quarter of the batter into each hole in the pan. Put half of the octopus pieces in each hole, then scatter half the pickled ginger and spring onions/scallions over the entire pan. Finally, pour over another quarter of the batter so it spreads across the flat surface of the pan. Reduce the heat to medium-low and cook without touching for 5 minutes.

Use bamboo skewers or chopsticks to push one side of the batter away from the rim of a hole. It will move easily if it's set underneath, if not then wait a little longer before trying again. Once the bottom is crispy, use chopsticks to rotate the balls 90 degrees so that any uncooked batter is underneath. Stuff any of the surrounding dough on the flat part of the pan inside the balls as you turn them. When the bottom becomes crispy again (after a minute or so), repeat the 90-degree rotation and stuffing process three more times in the same direction. At this point, turn the takoyaki around every which way, until the surface is golden all over and they are perfectly round! Using bamboo skewers, remove the takoyaki from the pan to serving plates or bamboo boats. Repeat the cooking process with the remaining ingredients to make a second batch.

Drizzle over the takoyaki sauce and mayonnaise, then sprinkle with bonito flakes and aonori before serving.

TARA KATSU

BREADED COD CHEEKS
WITH TOMATO SALSA

I was raised according to the traditional Japanese philosophy of learning how to appreciate food and trying not to waste it. We feel mottainai ('what a waste!') when produce is not used up properly. That's why I like to think beyond fillets with fish and use all parts of it. When it comes to sustainable fish, cod cheeks are amongst a chef's favourites. They're good value, boneless, skinless and surprisingly big! Their meat is firm and holds wonderfully prepared katsu style.

500 g/1 lb. 2 oz. fresh cod cheeks (available from fishmongers)
50 g/generous ⅓ cup plain/all-purpose flour
1 UK large/US extra-large egg, beaten
100 g/2⅓ cups panko breadcrumbs
750 ml/3¼ cups vegetable oil, for frying
salt and freshly ground black pepper

TOMATO SALSA
200 g/7 oz. cherry tomatoes, roughly chopped
20 g/¾ oz. red onion, finely chopped
small handful of fresh coriander/cilantro, roughly chopped
2 tbsp light soy sauce
1 tbsp freshly squeezed lime juice
1 tsp Worcestershire sauce
½ tsp golden caster/granulated sugar

mini bamboo skewers (optional)

SERVES 4–6

Season the cod cheeks with salt and pepper. Put the flour, beaten egg and panko breadcrumbs on three separate plates. Coat the cod cheeks first in the flour, then in the beaten egg and finally in the panko breadcrumbs, ensuring the cheeks are fully and evenly coated. Refrigerate for 15 minutes to allow the coating to set.

Meanwhile, make the salsa. Put the chopped tomatoes, red onion and coriander/cilantro in a bowl. Add the light soy sauce, lime juice, Worcestershire sauce and sugar. Mix well to combine and set aside.

To deep-fry the cod cheeks, heat the vegetable oil in a heavy-based saucepan to 170°C (340°F) over high heat. To check that the oil is ready, drop a few breadcrumbs into the oil. If they float to the surface and sizzle, then it means the oil is ready. Reduce the heat to medium to maintain the temperature.

Deep-fry the cod cheeks for about 3–4 minutes each, turning over a few times, until golden brown and crispy and the cod cheek is cooked through. Remove from the oil with a slotted spoon and transfer to a cooling rack.

Leave the cod cheeks to cool a little, then serve on small serving dishes with mini skewers, if you like, and a spoonful of the tomato salsa on top.

ASARI NO SAKAMUSHI

SAKE-STEAMED CLAMS WITH BUTTER

Asari no Sakamushi or sake-steamed clams is such a classic izakaya dish that I had to share it with you. Japanese cooks know that the best way to treat shellfish is not to mess around with it too much. These clams just need to be cooked quickly with a few aromatics and a splash of sake to bring out the sweetness. Once you have de-gritted the clams, this recipe is super quick but so tasty. It brings a sense of conviviality to the dinner table – so much so that it's this dish that bonds a son and his elderly mother back together in an episode of the wonderful TV series, *Midnight Diner*. This series is a great way to travel without moving and get a feel for the lives of regular people living in Tokyo.

500 g/1 lb. 2 oz. clams

1 tbsp sea salt flakes or ½ tbsp fine salt dissolved in 500 ml/2 cups plus 2 tbsp cold water (if using live clams)

100 ml/⅓ cup sake

1 garlic clove, finely chopped

100 g/3½ oz. cavolo nero (or you can use savoy cabbage)

1 tbsp soy sauce

1 tbsp unsalted butter

SERVES 4

Scrub the clams to remove any dirt from their shells.

If you bought clams from the supermarket/grocery store they will already have been 'purged' (the sand cleaned out of them), in this case you can skip the next step.

If you bought wild clams from the fishmonger, spread them out in a shallow, flat container without overlapping. Pour the salt water over to just cover the clams. Cover the container with a lid and refrigerate for at least 2 hours. The clams will 'purge' and spit out any sand trapped inside. Rinse well before continuing with the rest of the recipe.

Pour the sake into a large saucepan or casserole pan and add the clams to it. Sprinkle with the chopped garlic and place the cavolo nero on top. Cover with a lid and bring to the boil. When the clams open, reduce the heat to low and simmer for 3 more minutes. Discard any clams that have not opened.

Use a slotted spoon to gently take the clams and cavolo nero out of the pan and divide them between individual shallow serving bowls.

Season the sake cooking liquid in the pan with the soy sauce and butter. Warm through over gentle heat until the butter has melted, then pour the broth into each serving bowl over the clams. Serve while hot.

Pictured on pages 120–121

SABA NO NANBAN ZUKE

It's amazing to think that we owe this dish to the Portuguese and Spanish missionaries of the 14th century. While trying to spread the teachings of Christianity in Japan, they sparked a culinary revolution with their nanban ryori (southern barbarian cuisine), deep-frying fish and using the strong flavour of leek. In this dish, the mackerel is prepared nanban-style, which is deep-fried then marinated in a vinegar-based sauce. It's the perfect recipe for hot summer days when mackerel is at its best and it's slightly vinegared taste quenches our thirst. It's also an easy and delectable way to eat plenty of fish and vegetables whilst being surprisingly light for a fried dish.

4 mackerel fillets, skin on and pin-boned
2 tbsp plain/all-purpose flour
500 ml/2 cups plus 2 tbsp vegetable oil, for frying
salt

PICKLED VEGETABLES
½ onion, thinly sliced
1 carrot, peeled and cut into matchsticks
¼ red (bell) pepper, deseeded and cut into long strips
¼ fennel bulb, thinly sliced lengthways
150 ml/⅔ cup rice vinegar
3 tbsp light brown soft sugar
1 tbsp soy sauce
1 tbsp mirin
½ tsp salt
4 slices of orange

SERVES 4

Slice each mackerel fillet in half lengthwise. Sprinkle salt on the mackerel flesh and set aside for 10 minutes to draw out the excess moisture.

Meanwhile, place the sliced onion, carrot, red pepper and fennel into a flat, shallow baking dish or heatproof container.

Place the rice vinegar, brown sugar, soy sauce and mirin in a small saucepan with 100 ml/⅓ cup water and the salt. Bring to the boil, then pour the hot pickling liquid over the vegetables in the heatproof container.

Heat the vegetable oil in a heavy-based saucepan to 180°C (350°F) over high heat. To check that the oil is ready, stick the end of a wooden cooking chopstick (or heatproof spatula) into the oil. If it creates bubbles around the utensil, your oil is ready for frying. If it is bubbling hard, the oil is too hot; let it cool a bit and check the temperature again. Once the correct temperature has been reached, reduce the heat to medium to maintain it.

Just before cooking, wipe off any excess moisture from the mackerel, then coat with flour on both sides. Carefully place into the hot oil and deep-fry for 2–3 minutes, turning once, until crispy. Remove the mackerel with a slotted spoon and transfer to a cooling rack to drain the excess oil.

While the mackerel is still hot, transfer it to the container with the pickling vegetables and gently mix them together. Add the orange slices and leave to cool for at least 20 minutes before refrigerating overnight.

If you have used the freshest mackerel, you can keep nanban zuke in the fridge for up to 3 days – the longer you leave it, the better it tastes!

Pictured on pages 120–121

SAKE NO SHOCHU ZUKE

I prefer my salmon lightly cured compared to conventional recipes which often use longer curing times. This makes it light in texture and not overly salty. Here, I've served it with a slightly sweet miso-mustard sauce, which I think goes particularly well. You can also serve this on its own or with sliced sourdough bread for a more filling bite to eat. Drink-wise, it goes down a treat with a shochu soda-wari (shochu with carbonated water) or a dry sake.

20 g/¾ oz. fine salt (4% of the weight of the salmon)

20 g/¾ oz. golden caster/granulated sugar (4% of the weight of the salmon)

500 g/1 lb. 2 oz. skin-on centre cut sashimi-grade salmon fillet, pin-boned

10 g/⅓ oz. fresh dill, finely chopped

10 g/⅓ oz. fresh coriander/cilantro, chopped

grated zest of ½ orange or lemon

2½ tbsp shochu (or 2 tbsp gin)

½ red onion, thinly sliced and soaked in cold water for 10 minutes, drained

Miso Mustard Sauce (see page 38), to serve

SERVES 4

Mix the fine salt and golden caster/granulated sugar together and spread out on a wide, flat tray. Add the salmon to the tray and turn it over until coated on all sides in the salt and sugar.

Place the salmon inside an airtight container. Add the dill, coriander/cilantro and orange or lemon zest and spread evenly around the fish. Finally, evenly sprinkle in the shochu. Seal the lid of the container and refrigerate for at least 2 hours and up to 24 hours.

Once the salmon is cured, remove it from the container, drain any liquid and pat it dry. Carefully remove the salmon skin, then use a long, sharp knife to cut the salmon into thin slices on the diagonal.

Serve with sliced red onion and the miso mustard sauce.

NOTE *If you haven't served all the cured salmon and want to keep the rest, wrap the fish in a clean cloth or kitchen towel, place it back inside the airtight container with the orange zest and herbs and refrigerate for up to 3 more days.*

Pictured on pages 120–121

SUZUKI NO YUAN YAKI

FRIED MARINATED SEA BASS

Yuan yaki is a traditional grilling (yaki) cooking method, not dissimilar to teriyaki. However, this marinade has the additional ingredient of citrus juice to make the dish extra refreshing. Yuan refers to the name of a famous chajin (master of tea ceremony) of the Edo period who, being a gourmet, came up with the idea of marinating fish with soy sauce, sake and for the first time in Japanese cuisine, mirin! It's such a no-fuss, quick recipe, but it always tastes so special.

2 skin-on sea bass fillets (about 360 g/12½ oz. combined weight), pin-boned
salt
½ tbsp vegetable oil
2 thin slices of unsalted butter
½ lime, thinly sliced

YUAN SAUCE
2 tbsp soy sauce
2 tbsp mirin
1 tbsp sake
1 tbsp freshly squeezed lime juice
1 tsp light brown soft sugar

large frying pan/skillet with a lid

SERVES 4

Place the sea bass skin-side down on a chopping board and sprinkle a pinch of salt onto the flesh. Set aside for 20 minutes to draw out the excess moisture.

Meanwhile, to make the yuan sauce, mix all the ingredients together in a small bowl. Set aside.

Wipe off any excess moisture from the flesh of the fish, then slice each fillet widthways diagonally into three pieces to create a wider surface area.

Pour the oil into a large frying pan/skillet over medium heat. Add the sea bass skin-side down and fry for 1–2 minutes until the skin is slightly browned. Flip the fillets over and cook the flesh side for 1 minute.

Pour the yuan sauce over the sea bass, then cover the pan with a lid, reduce the heat to medium-low and simmer for about 2 minutes until the sauce has mostly reduced and become glossy.

Uncover the pan and add a thin slice of butter to the top of each fish fillet. Let the butter melt and coat the fish, then serve on individual plates, garnished with slices of fresh lime.

Pictured on pages 120–121

HIYA JIRU

冷や汁

*COLD MISO SOUP WITH
SMOKED MACKEREL*

This is probably the friendliest sounding recipe you've ever encountered!
Conversely, hiya actually refers to 'cold' and jiru to 'soup' in Japanese.
It is one of the regional dishes of Kyushu, Japan's southern region where
I grew up. The summers are very hot and humid there and this soup is the
panacea to the soaring heat. Make sure you add plenty of herbs so it's extra
refreshing, as well as ice cubes to chill the soup!

200 g/7 oz. boneless smoked
mackerel fillets, skin removed,
broken into small flakes
½ cucumber, thinly sliced
¼ tsp fine salt
200 g/7 oz. dried somen noodles

SESAME MISO PASTE
30 g/1 oz. toasted white sesame
seeds
60 g/2 oz. white miso
60 ml/¼ cup mirin
400 ml/1⅔ cups chilled Dashi of
your choice (see pages 32–33)

TOPPINGS
2 spring onions/scallions, thinly
sliced
2 myoga ginger (Japanese ginger),
thinly sliced
4 fresh green shiso leaves,
thinly sliced

SERVES 4

Place the sliced cucumber in a bowl and sprinkle with the salt. Lightly rub
the salt into the cucumber slices, then leave for 10 minutes to draw out
the excess moisture. Use your hands to squeeze and drain the water from
the cucumber, then set aside.

Grind the sesame seeds to a fine paste in a suribachi (Japanese grinder)
or a pestle and mortar. Place the paste in a bowl and add the white miso
and mirin. Mix them together to make a smooth paste.

You now want to char the paste to create an aromatic flavour. Scoop
the paste out using a heatproof spatula. Turn the spatula upside down
(the paste is thick so it won't fall off) and carefully hold it over the flame
of a hob/stove-top for 30 seconds or until the surface of the paste
browns. Or, preheat the grill/broiler to 200°C (400°F) or to medium-
high. Spread the paste out on a heatproof grill pan and grill/broil for
3 minutes until the top browns.

Place the charred sesame miso paste back in the bowl and mix with
the chilled dashi until dissolved. Set aside.

For the noodles, bring a large saucepan of water to the boil. Add the
noodles and stir gently to disentangle the bundles. Boil according to the
packet instructions, adding some cold water if the noodles start to boil
over. Drain and immediately rinse the noodles under cold running water
in a sieve/strainer to stop the cooking process. Drain well again.

To serve, divide the noodles between serving bowls. Sprinkle over the
cucumber and smoked mackerel flakes, then pour the soup over the top.
Garnish with the spring onions/scallions, myoga ginger and shiso leaves.
You can also add ice cubes to the soup to make it extra refreshing when
it is hot! Serve straight away.

KANI ZOSUI

Zosui is something between a risotto and a porridge. It is usually enjoyed at the end of a nomikai or work drinks party to finish the meal. There are various types of zosui, some being soupy and others a thicker consistency. I prefer the latter, which I'm sharing with you in this recipe. This dish is enjoyed at the end of the meal because of its digestive properties. The rice is simmered longer than usual and is very delicate in flavour. Especially prepared in winter, it will warm up your body at the end of a cold day. This is proper, healthy comfort food.

400 ml/1⅔ cups Kombu & Katsuobushi Dashi (see page 33)
250 g/9 oz. cooked rice (next-day rice is even better for this, see pages 30–31)
1 tbsp sake
1 tbsp light soy sauce
2 tsp mirin
150 g/5½ oz. white and brown crab meat
1 egg, beaten
salt

TO SERVE
50 g/1¾ oz. salmon roe
small handful of coriander/cilantro leaves

SERVES 4

Bring the katsuobushi dashi to the boil in a large saucepan or Japanese donabe hot pot.

Add the cooked rice, sake, light soy sauce and mirin. Cover with the lid and simmer for 5 minutes over low heat.

Add the crab meat, stir and cover with the lid again. Simmer over low heat for a further 5 minutes. The consistency should be getting towards something like a thick porridge.

Towards the end of the simmering time, pour the beaten egg over the top of the rice, then replace the lid and simmer for a final 2 minutes.

Stir gently to mix the egg with the rice and season with a little salt if necessary. Serve in individual serving bowls, topped with salmon roe and coriander/cilantro leaves.

野菜
VEGETABLES

枝豆ペペロンチーノ
EDAMAME WITH CHILLI & GARLIC

EDAMAME PEPPERONCINO

I included a classic wasabi edamame recipe in my cookbook, *Atsuko's Japanese Kitchen*, as I know that people love the combination of edamame and spice. Here is another version that takes you to Italy with the addition of chilli and garlic.

500 g/1 lb. 2 oz. frozen edamame
   beans in pods
1 tbsp olive oil
2 garlic cloves, finely chopped
2 red chillies, deseeded and
   very finely chopped
salt

SERVES 4

Cook the edamame beans in 2 litres/quarts of boiling salted water for 2 minutes. Drain well.

Heat a large frying pan/skillet over medium-low heat. Add the olive oil, garlic, chillies and a pinch of salt. Let the oil heat up and infuse with all the flavours for 2 minutes.

Add the edamame and stir to dress them in the oil. Serve hot.

Pictured on page 132

とうもろこしの味噌バター焼き
MISO & CHIVE BUTTER SWEETCORN

TOMOROKOSHI NO MISO BUTTER YAKI

Grilled corn is a typical Japanese street food and, to me, it's the perfect embodiment of a hot summer's day: the sweet smoky smell, the golden colour of the cob slightly charred... slather on some miso butter and it's a stairway to heaven!

4 sweetcorn cobs/ears (buy these still
   in their green husks if possible)
big pinch of salt

MISO & CHIVE BUTTER
60 g/½ stick butter, diced
2 tbsp white miso
10 g/⅓ oz. fresh chives, finely chopped
2 tsp maple syrup
freshly squeezed juice of ½ lemon

MAKES 4

Leave the butter out of the fridge to soften for 1 hour. Or, if you are in a rush, you can put the diced butter in a bowl of lukewarm water for 10 minutes to warm up, then drain (a tip from Mary Berry!).

Boil the sweetcorn cobs/ears in a large pan of salted water for 5 minutes until just tender. Drain and leave until cool enough to handle, then remove the husks and any hairs from the corn if needed.

Preheat the grill/broiler to 240°C (460°F) or to the high setting.

In a small bowl, mix the butter to loosen it, then mix in the white miso and chives.

Put the corn on a grill/broiler tray with foil under it. Spread half the miso butter over the corn and grill/broil for 5 minutes, turning a couple of times, until evenly charred. Dot over the rest of the butter and drizzle with maple syrup and lemon juice to serve.

たたききゅうり
SMACKED CUCUMBER

TATAKI KYURI

We're used to eating cucumbers either raw or pickled, but this recipe uses the cucumber in a slightly different way, adding interest without compromising the natural texture and flavour.

1 English cucumber
1 tbsp light soy sauce
1 tbsp rice vinegar
1 tbsp toasted sesame oil
1 tsp light brown soft sugar
¼ tsp garlic purée/paste
toasted white sesame seeds
shichimi spice mix, to taste (optional)

SERVES 4

Place the cucumber on a chopping board and smack it with a rolling pin so it splits open. Use your hands to rip the cucumber into bite-sized pieces, about 2.5 cm/1 inch.

Mix the rest of the ingredients together in a bowl. Toss in the cucumber and stir to coat in the dressing.

Refrigerate for at least 10 minutes before serving chilled with shichimi spice mix, if you like.

トマトのバジルポン酢和え
TOMATO, BASIL & PONZU SALAD

TOMATO NO BASIL PONZU AE

This may come as a surprise, but the Japanese are avid tomato eaters! Local growers pride themselves on their tasty varieties. To balance the sweetness, I like to serve them with a refreshing ponzu dressing.

400 g/14 oz. mixed tomatoes
½ red chicory/endive, thinly sliced
2 tbsp soy sauce
2 tbsp mirin
1 tbsp rice vinegar
freshly squeezed juice of ½ lime
1 garlic clove, thickly sliced
15 g/½ oz. fresh basil leaves, stems
   removed, thinly sliced

SERVES 4

Roughly cut the smaller tomatoes in half and dice the larger tomatoes into chunks. Place them in a shallow bowl or glass/ceramic dish with the chicory/endive and gently toss both ingredients together.

Mix the soy sauce, mirin, rice vinegar and lime juice together in a cup. Add the sliced garlic and stir well. Pour the dressing over the tomatoes and sprinkle with the sliced basil.

Refrigerate for at least 10 minutes before serving chilled. Remove the sliced garlic before you eat.

NASU NO NIBITASHI

*AUBERGINE/EGGPLANT WITH
SESAME SOY SAUCE*

Nibitashi means 'simmer and soak' and is a traditional cooking method where vegetables are immersed and cooked in dashi broth. This aubergine/eggplant version of nibitashi is such a popular home cooking dish, and particularly enjoyed in the summer when aubergines are in season. Usually in this dish, aubergines are fried, but I prefer to steam them whole. This way, they keep their moisture and all their flavours and dashi needn't be added. It's important here to grind your sesame seeds to a paste to bind the sauce. You can easily do this using a food processor or a suribachi, the traditional Japanese grinder.

2 aubergines/eggplant
30 g/1 oz. toasted white sesame
    seeds
2 tbsp toasted sesame oil
2 tbsp soy sauce
2 tbsp mirin
1 tsp light brown soft sugar

TO SERVE
1 tsp chilli oil
1 tsp peeled and finely grated
    fresh ginger
pinch of fresh chives,
    finely chopped

SERVES 4

Peel the skins off the aubergines/eggplant but leave the stalks on for now (they can be removed easily when cooked).

Bring a shallow layer of water to the boil in a large saucepan (enough to cover the aubergines/eggplant by about a third). Place the whole aubergines/eggplant in the pan, cover with a lid and let them steam for 15 minutes, turning once halfway through.

Meanwhile, to make the sesame soy sauce, grind the toasted white sesame seeds to a grainy paste in a food processor, spice grinder or traditional Japanese tool called a suribachi. Put the ground sesame seeds in a bowl with the toasted sesame oil, soy sauce, mirin and brown sugar. Stir together and set aside.

Once the aubergines/eggplant are cooked, remove them from the pan and leave to cool until you can easily handle them. Tear the aubergines/eggplant apart lengthwise with your fingers into pieces and remove and discard the stems. Place in a serving dish, then stir the sesame soy sauce again and spoon it over the aubergines/eggplant to dress.

Serve the aubergines/eggplant slightly warm or keep in the fridge and serve chilled when you are ready – both ways work. Just before serving, drizzle with chilli oil and scatter over the grated ginger and chopped chives.

ししとうの焼き浸し
MARINADED PADRÓN PEPPERS

SHISHITOU NO YAKIBITASHI

In Japan we don't have Padrón peppers, but we do have their similar cousins, shishitou peppers. Yaki means grilled or fried, and bitashi refers to the marinade. I like to skewer these to make them easier to handle when turning and frying.

250 g/9 oz. (about 16) Padrón peppers
   or shishitou peppers
vegetable oil, for coating the peppers

OHITASHI MARINADE
100 ml/⅓ cup Dashi of your choice
   (see pages 32–33)
2 tbsp soy sauce
2 tbsp mirin

8 x 15-cm/6-inch wooden skewers,
soaked in cold water for 15 minutes

SERVES 4

Place four peppers in a line on a chopping board and skewer them with two skewers. Repeat for the remaining peppers and skewers. Rub a little vegetable oil over all the peppers, then set aside.

To make the ohitashi marinade, mix the dashi, soy sauce and mirin together in a tray with a rim.

Heat a ridged stove-top griddle pan/grill pan or frying pan/skillet over medium-high heat. Depending on the size of your pan, you may need to cook these in two or three batches. Add the peppers to the pan and cook for 3–4 minutes, turning halfway through, until both sides are nicely browned.

Dip the peppers on their skewers in the ohitashi marinade while they are still hot. Leave the peppers in the marinade for a minimum of 30 minutes at room temperature or leave to cool fully and then chill in the fridge for up to 2 days until ready to eat.

のり塩ポテト焼き
FRIED POTATOES WITH NORI

NORI SHIO POTATO YAKI

This is one of my family's favourite potato dishes. I was inspired by Norishio, a popular Japanese seaweed and salt flavoured potato crisp/chip.

400 g/14 oz. new potatoes
4 tbsp plain/all-purpose flour (or
   cornflour/cornstarch for gluten-free)
2 tbsp vegetable oil
¼ tsp dashi powder of your choice
   (or use powdered stock/bouillon)
pinch of salt
2 tbsp aonori seaweed flakes

26–28-cm/10–11-inch frying pan/skillet
with lid

SERVES 4

Cut the potatoes into bite-sized pieces of equal thickness – cut any small potatoes in half and any large ones into wedges. Toss the potatoes in the flour or cornstarch to give an even coating.

Pour the oil into a large frying pan/skillet set over high heat. Add the potatoes when the oil is hot, then turn the heat down to medium and fry for 3 minutes, turning the potatoes a couple of times, until browned on all sides.

Turn the heat down to low, then cover the pan with a lid and steam the potatoes for 10 minutes.

Remove the lid and turn the heat back up to medium-high. Add the dashi powder and salt. Stir-fry the potatoes for 2 minutes until crispy.

Just before you are ready to serve, add the aonori seaweed flakes and shake the pan to evenly distribute them among the potatoes. Serve hot.

Pictured on page 135

HANATABA TEMPURA

If you've ever wondered if it was possible to make ultra-crispy tempura without using egg or wheat... the answer is YES! I needed to find a great alternative recipe for the all-time favourite dish that is tempura, suitable for my clients with egg or gluten allergies. Once I started experimenting with rice flour, I was amazed at how long-lasting the crispness was, and how easy the method was! There is no need to fuss over not mixing this dough too much, for example. The trickiest part of this recipe is arranging the vegetables neatly in appealing bouquets using nori strips to tie them up. Once you've done the first one you'll easily get the hang of it, and I can assure you your guests will be wowed by your presentation.

1 carrot (plus the carrot top if it comes with it), peeled and cut into julienne (matchsticks)

1 baby courgette/zucchini, sliced lengthwise into julienne (matchsticks)

3 Tenderstem broccoli/broccolini, leaves removed from the stem, torn into branches

6 baby corn, cut in half lengthwise

¼ red (bell) pepper, deseeded and cut into strips

½ avocado, peeled, stoned/pitted and cut into slim wedges

½ nori sheet, cut into 12 long strips (10 x 1.5 cm/4 x ⅝ inch)

750 ml/3¼ cups vegetable oil, for frying

your favourite Flavoured Mayo, to serve (see pages 40–41)

TEMPURA BATTER
50 g/generous ⅓ cup rice flour
¼ tsp fine salt

MAKES 12

For the tempura batter, place the rice flour and salt in a medium mixing bowl. Gradually whisk in 100 ml/⅓ cup cold water until well combined into a smooth batter. Set aside.

To prepare the vegetable 'bouquets', pick up 4–5 different prepared vegetable strips and bunch them together neatly. Wrap a strip of nori around the middle, then dab the end of the nori with a little batter and press down to seal it. Gently spread out one end of the vegetables so it looks like a little a bouquet!

Heat the vegetable oil in a heavy-based saucepan to 180°C (350°F) over high heat.

To check that the oil is ready, drop a little bit of batter into the oil. If it floats to the surface with a gentle sizzle, it's ready. Reduce the heat to medium to maintain the temperature.

Gently stir the tempura batter, then dip each vegetable bouquet into the batter to give an even coating before carefully lowering into the hot oil. Deep-fry the bouquets in two batches of six for 2–3 minutes, turning them over a couple of times as they cook.

Remove with a slotted spoon and transfer to a cooling rack to drain any excess oil. Serve the tempura bouquets warm with your favourite mayo dip on the side.

HOSOI HARUMAKI

Harumaki are literally spring (haru) rolls (maki) and they fit into the wafu-chuka (Japanese-Chinese) category of dishes. They're crisp on the outside but soft and flavourful on the inside. You can also make them with Jerusalem artichokes. The combination of Jerusalem artichoke with truffle mayo is to die for!

250 g/9 oz. medium white potatoes
1 vegetable stock/bouillon cube
30 g/1 oz. mayonnaise
10 g/⅓ oz. grated Cheddar
    (optional)
pinch of ground white pepper
pinch of salt
10 harumaki spring roll wrappers
    (19-cm/7½-inch square)
2 tbsp plain/all-purpose flour,
    mixed with 2 tbsp water,
    for brushing
20 coriander/cilantro leaves
750 ml/3¼ cups vegetable oil,
    for frying
Truffle Mayo (see page 41),
    to serve

MAKES 10

Put the potatoes in a medium saucepan, cover with water and bring to the boil. Add the stock/bouillon cube, then reduce the heat to medium-high and simmer for 15 minutes until the potatoes are cooked. Drain and leave in a colander until completely dry and warm but cool enough to handle.

Peel the skins off the boiled potatoes and discard. Dice the potatoes, then put them in a food processor with the mayonnaise, grated cheese (if using), white pepper and salt. Blend to make a thick, smooth paste. Alternatively, you can mash the ingredients together in a bowl.

Place the harumaki wrappers on a flat work surface in front of you in a diamond position. Use a teaspoon to position the potato paste in a thin horizontal line, about 5 cm/2 inches above the bottom corner on each wrapper from edge to edge.

Brush the top corner of a wrapper with a little of the flour and water mixture. Fold the bottom corner of the wrapper up and tightly over the potato filling, then start rolling the wrapper up, removing as much air as possible, with the potato encased inside. Stop halfway and fold both ends of the pasty in. Place two coriander/cilantro leaves in the middle, then finish rolling to the top corner and seal it down. Repeat for the remaining wrappers and filling.

To fry the spring rolls, heat the vegetable oil in a heavy-based saucepan to 160°C (320°F) over high heat. To check that the oil is ready, carefully dip a spring roll in the oil. If it gently sizzles, then it means the oil is ready. Reduce the heat to medium-low to maintain the temperature. Deep-fry the harumaki in two batches, for 3 minutes each, turning over a few times, until browned and crispy. Remove from the hot oil with tongs and transfer to a cooling rack to drain and cool slightly.

Serve warm with some truffle mayo for dipping.

TSUMETAI PINK
NO SOUP

This is a very simple cauliflower-based soup before a tiny piece of beetroot/beet is added! The colour then turns a gorgeous cherry-blossom hue, rather than an intense pink. As well as being delicious and refreshing, the colour makes this soup rather unique, and it often makes people smile.

1 tbsp olive oil
80 g/2¾ oz. onion, finely chopped
80 g/2¾ oz. celery, finely chopped
1 garlic clove, thinly sliced
450 g/1 lb. cauliflower, cut into florets
600 ml/2½ cups hot Kombu & Katsuobushi Dashi (see page 33) or vegetable stock/broth
6 g/¼ oz. cooked beetroot/beet, cut into small cubes
200 ml/scant 1 cup single/light cream
1 tsp sea salt

TO SERVE
extra cooked beetroot/beet, thinly sliced and cut into a pattern using a mini cookie cutter
extra single/light cream, for drizzling

**MAKES 8 SMALL GLASSES
(125 ML/½ CUP EACH)**

Heat the oil in a large saucepan over medium heat. Add the onion and celery to the pan and fry for 7 minutes, stirring occasionally, until softened.

Add the garlic and cauliflower, then cook for 2 more minutes, stirring to coat the cauliflower in the oil. Add the dashi to the pan and bring to the boil. Reduce the heat, cover the pan with a lid and simmer for 10 minutes until the cauliflower is tender.

Add the cooked beetroot/beet to the soup, then blitz the mixture until smooth using a hand-held stick blender or by transferring the contents of the pan to a food processor. Add the single/light cream, little by little, and blend again – you may not need to use all the cream depending on how you prefer the colour (I prefer a pale cherry-blossom pink).

Season with the salt, then leave the soup to cool before chilling in the fridge for a minimum of 2 hours.

Serve the chilled soup in small individual glasses for a cocktail party. Garnish with cut pieces of beetroot/beet just before serving (if you leave it too long, the colour from the garnish will darken the soup). Finish by drizzling over a few drops of cream and dragging a cocktail stick/toothpick through them to make pretty patterns, if you like.

TSUMETAI EDAMAME
NO SOUP

冷たい枝豆のスープ
CHILLED EDAMAME SOUP

Celebrate the summer with this light and refreshing, chilled edamame soup.
When it's hot outside, you don't feel like eating too much or getting hot and sweaty
in the kitchen. This recipe is so quick and easy to whip up and just hits the spot.
It looks elegant when served in small glasses at your dinner party alongside the
Chilled Pink Soup (see page 143) for a fabulous colour contrast.

1 tbsp extra virgin olive oil,
   plus extra for garnishing
25 g/¾ oz. onion, finely chopped
200 g/7 oz. frozen shelled
   edamame beans
400 ml/1⅔ cups Dashi of your
   choice (see pages 32–33)
1 tsp light soy sauce
1 tbsp sake
salt
fresh mint leaves, to garnish

**MAKES 4 SMALL GLASSES
(150 ML/⅔ CUP EACH)**

Heat the extra virgin olive oil in a medium saucepan over medium heat.
Add the onion and fry for 7 minutes, stirring occasionally, until softened.

Add the edamame beans and the dashi to the pan and bring to the boil.
Reduce the heat, cover the pan with a lid and simmer for 5 minutes until
the beans are cooked.

Turn off the heat and leave the soup to cool a little. Blitz the mixture until
smooth using a hand-held stick blender or by transferring the contents of
the pan to a food processor.

Add the light soy sauce, sake and salt to taste. Return the soup to the pan
if you need to, then heat for 2 more minutes over medium heat to infuse
the flavours. Leave the soup to cool, then chill in the fridge for a minimum
of 2 hours before serving.

Serve in small individual glasses for a cocktail party. Drizzle the soups with
a little extra virgin olive oil and garnish with mint leaves.

Pictured on page 143

NAMA HARIMAKI

Summer rolls have never been so aptly named than with this recipe! Crunchy strips of vegetables and fresh, fragrant herbs, all wrapped in a light rice paper roll and decorated with edible flowers. Not only do they look beautiful, but they are surprisingly easy to make. Dip them in the two sauces below, but also in any other dips like the Rainbow Dips (see pages 56–57) for some striking colours.

8 round rice paper wrappers
(22 cm/8¾ inches in diameter)

FILLING
200 g/7 oz. Tenderstem broccoli/
  broccolini
80 g/2¾ oz. green beans
80 g/2¾ oz. mixed baby leaf salad,
  such as baby lettuce, rocket/
  arugula, red sorrel, etc.
20 g/¾ oz. mixed fresh herbs, such
  as mint, shiso, basil, coriander/
  cilantro, etc.
1 carrot, peeled and sliced into
  julienne (matchsticks)
16 seasonal edible flowers, such
  as viola, dahlia, nasturtium, etc.

FISH DIPPING SAUCE
2 tbsp fish sauce or soy sauce
1 tbsp rice vinegar
1 tbsp freshly squeezed lemon juice
2 tsp golden caster/granulated
  sugar
1 tsp toasted sesame oil
1 red chilli, deseeded, finely chopped

PEANUT BUTTER DIPPING SAUCE
3 tbsp smooth peanut butter
1 tbsp sweet white miso
4 tbsp mirin
3 tbsp light soy sauce
1½ tbsp rice vinegar
1 large garlic clove

MAKES 8

Cook the broccoli and green beans together for 2 minutes in a large saucepan of boiling salted water. Immediately drain and plunge the vegetables into a bowl of ice-cold water to stop the cooking process. Drain well again and set aside.

For the rice paper wrappers, fill a shallow, rimmed container (such as a baking pan) halfway with cold water. It should be large enough to fit a rice paper wrapper inside. Dip a wrapper into the water, making sure it is wet all over, then remove from the water and place it gently on a clean, flat work surface. Leave it for a minute to reconstitute.

To fill the rice paper, place some leaves and herbs horizontally in the middle of the wrapper, leaving some space at either edge. Top these with 1–2 broccoli stems, 2–3 green beans and a small bunch of sliced carrot sticks. Place two of the edible flowers at the top so you will be able to clearly see them through the rice paper.

Start rolling the rice paper up by folding the bottom of the wrapper up and over to cover the fillings, making sure they are all tucked neatly inside. Fold in both ends of the rice paper wrapper, then continue tightly but gently rolling up to the end of the wrapper. Cover with a clean, damp cloth and repeat for the remaining rice paper wrappers and fillings.

Leave the summer rolls to settle under the damp cloth for 5 minutes.

Meanwhile, mix the fish dipping sauce ingredients together in a small bowl and set aside.

Blitz all the peanut butter dipping sauce ingredients together, either in a food processor or in a jar using a hand-held stick blender. If the texture is too thick, then add a couple of tablespoons of water to dilute it to a dipping sauce consistency.

Cut each summer roll widthways into four portions to serve them as bite-sized morsels. Serve with both dipping sauces.

Pictured on pages 146–147

KINOKO NO MISO GURATAN

When autumn approaches, one craves something comforting and creamy, and this recipe just hits the spot! It's also a celebration of seasonality, which is at the core of Japanese food philosophy. Nowadays, you can get a good selection of Japanese mushrooms in big supermarkets/grocery stores. You'll enjoy their different textures and shapes in this recipe. If you don't like turnip or have trouble sourcing it, daikon or potatoes work perfectly well too, using the same cooking method.

1 turnip, peeled and diced into bite-sized chunks

200 g/7 oz. mixed mushrooms of your choice (I used shimeji, eryngii, enoki and shiitake)

1 tbsp olive oil

2 tsp butter

80 g/3 oz. leek, thinly sliced

2 tbsp sake

150 ml/⅔ cup double/heavy cream

2 tbsp white miso

40 g/scant ½ cup grated Cheddar

3 tbsp panko breadcrumbs

SERVES 4

Preheat the grill/broiler to 200°C (400°F) or to medium-high.

Bring 1.5 litres/quarts of water to the boil in a medium-sized saucepan. Add the turnip and cook for about 5 minutes or until cooked thoroughly. Drain well.

Meanwhile, trim the mushrooms and remove the woody parts from the bottom. Cut any larger ones into bite-sized pieces.

Heat a medium saucepan (ideally ovenproof) over high heat. Add the olive oil and butter. When the butter has melted, add the leek and stir-fry for 1 minute, then add the mushrooms and continue stir-frying for another 2 minutes.

Add the cooked turnip and sake. Cover the pan with a lid, reduce the heat to medium and steam for 1 minute. Add the cream and miso and stir constantly to dissolve the miso in the cream. Simmer until the cream is reduced by half.

If you are not using an ovenproof pan, transfer the creamy mushroom mixture to an ovenproof baking dish. Sprinkle over the grated cheese then the panko breadcrumbs. Transfer the gratin to the preheated grill/broiler and cook until the cheese has melted and the breadcrumbs are golden brown. Serve hot.

KAISOU NO CONG YOU BING

*SEAWEED & SPRING ONION/
SCALLION FLATBREADS WITH
CHILLI OIL DIPPING SAUCE*

I love a table with a loaf of bread or flatbreads to share! It encapsulates the idea of communality and breaking bread with friends and family. I was inspired by the Chinese street food Cong You Bing (spring onion/scallion pancakes) for this recipe. They're essentially stuffed flatbreads, flaky on the outside and chewy on the inside. For a Japanese twist, I stuff mine with aonori and wakame seaweed alongside the spring onions/scallions for extra umami flavour. It's so simple but, especially when served with the chilli oil dipping sauce, it's highly addictive!

200 g/1½ cups plain/all-purpose flour, plus extra for dusting
¼ tsp sea salt
150 ml/⅔ cup boiling water
approx. 60 ml/¼ cup vegetable oil
50 g/1¾ oz. spring onions/scallions, thinly sliced
2 tbsp dried wakame, soaked in water for 3 minutes, drained well and roughly chopped
2 tbsp aonori seaweed flakes

CHILLI OIL DIPPING SAUCE
2 tbsp soy sauce
2 tbsp mirin
2 tbsp rice vinegar
2 tsp chilli oil

MAKES 4 FLATBREADS

Sift the flour into a large mixing bowl. Add the salt to the boiling water in a heatproof jug/pitcher and mix well until it has dissolved. Slowly pour the salted boiling water into the flour, stirring gently using chopsticks or a spatula, until the mixture comes together into a dough. Use your hands to bring it together at the end.

Lightly dust a work surface with flour. Tip the dough out onto the floured work surface and knead it through for 5 minutes until smooth. Return the dough to the bowl, cover it with a clean, damp cloth and leave it to rest for 30 minutes at room temperature.

Meanwhile, mix all the ingredients for the chilli oil dipping sauce together in a small bowl and set aside.

Unwrap the dough and divide it into four portions. Dust the work surface with a little more flour, then press a piece of dough flat onto the work surface using your palm.

Use a rolling pin to roll the dough out to a very thin, roughly rectangular shape, approx. 21-29 cm/8¼-11¼ inches long. Cover the rest of the dough with clingfilm/plastic wrap or a damp cloth to prevent it from drying out as you work.

Recipe continued overleaf >>

Brush 1 tbsp of the vegetable oil onto the surface of the dough, then evenly sprinkle it with a quarter of the spring onions/scallions, wakame and aonori flakes.

Roll the dough up gently into a sausage shape with the filling inside, then roll the sausage up into a spiral shape. Set aside, cover and repeat for the remaining dough and filling.

Just before starting to cook, use the rolling pin to gently roll each dough spiral out as thinly as possible to make a flat, round pancake shape, roughly 20–22 cm/8–8¾ inches in diameter.

Heat a frying pan/skillet over high heat. Add ½ tbsp vegetable oil to the frying pan/skillet, then place a pancake on it. Turn the heat to medium-low and cook for about 4–5 minutes in total, flipping halfway through, until both sides of the pancake are golden and browned. Remove the pancake to a plate and cook the rest of the dough in the same way.

Serve the pancakes hot with the chilli oil dipping sauce.

NOTE *If you don't want to cook the pancakes straight away, you can spread a little more oil onto the surface to preserve the moisture and layer the pancakes between baking parchment. They will keep at room temperature for a few hours or overnight in the fridge. Use a little less oil when cooking.*

CHIGIRI SALADA

This is the ultimate hassle-free salad dish! You don't even need a knife, just use your hands to tear the ingredients. The only thing that might take a little time is the deep-frying of the gyoza skins. If you don't have any or don't feel like doing it, you can easily replace them with croutons or fried shallots – something light that will go with the crunchy nori – it's all about adding a crispy texture to your salad. The miso ginger dressing gives an important richness to the recipe.

2 tbsp dried mixed seaweeds (such as wakame, agar, aka tsunomata)
½ iceberg lettuce
250 ml/1 cup vegetable oil, for deep-frying
4 gyoza skins
1 nori sheet
Miso Ginger Dressing, to serve (see page 35)

SERVES 4

Soak the dried seaweeds in a bowl of cold water for 10–15 minutes. Drain well and keep in the fridge until you are ready to use them.

Remove the root and outer leaves from the lettuce and tear the rest into bite-sized pieces. Soak the lettuce in a bowl of cold water for 10 minutes to make it crisp, then drain well and keep in the fridge until you are ready to use it.

To deep-fry the gyoza skins, heat the vegetable oil in a large, heavy-based frying pan/skillet to 180°C (350°F) over medium-high heat. To check that the oil is ready, drop a gyoza wrapper into the oil. If it floats to the surface and gently sizzles, the oil is ready. Add the gyoza skins, then reduce the heat to medium to maintain the temperature. Fry for about 30 seconds until they turn golden brown, then turn over and fry the other side for 30 seconds until golden brown. Remove the gyoza skins from the hot oil with a slotted spoon and drain well on a cooling rack.

Place the soaked and drained lettuce leaves and seaweed in a serving bowl. Give the miso ginger dressing a shake, then pour over the salad and gently toss together. Lightly crush the fried gyoza skins over the salad, then tear over the nori. Serve immediately.

NOTE *There is no need for a knife or peeler to remove the skin from fresh ginger, simply use a teaspoon. Hold a teaspoon close to the neck and cover the bowl part with your index finger. Grab some ginger in your other hand, then use the tip of the teaspoon to scrape the skin off from top to bottom. Use your index finger to help move the tip of the spoon. You do not need to cut off the lumps.*

豆腐と卵
TOFU & EGGS

HIYA YAKKO SANSHU

This traditional dish brings me back to sweltering summer days in Japan when you don't feel much like cooking. The velvety texture of the tofu helps the body cool down while giving it the right nourishment to feel satisfied. It is also the easiest no-cook recipe that can be whipped up quickly: it's essentially a chilled block or scoop of tofu with toppings. People love it so much they will make it at home but also order it at izakayas to share between friends. Just be sure to get good quality tofu as it is, after all, the star ingredient.

CLASSIC TOFU

400 g/14 oz. medium-firm tofu, drained and patted dry
1 tbsp ground white sesame seeds
1 spring onion/scallion, finely chopped, then soaked in cold water for 10 minutes to remove bitterness, drained
pinch of bonito flakes (katsuobushi)
3 tbsp Banno Sauce (see page 35)

SERVES 4

Dice the tofu into four cubes, then place on individual serving plates. Garnish the tofu with ground sesame seeds, spring onions/scallions and bonito flakes. Pour the banno sauce over the tofu before serving.

YAKUMI TOFU

400 g/14 oz. medium-firm tofu, drained and patted dry

PEANUT BUTTER SAUCE
3 tbsp smooth peanut butter
1 tbsp sweet white miso
4 tbsp mirin
3 tbsp light soy sauce
1½ tbsp rice vinegar
1 large garlic clove

YAKUMI TOPPINGS
1 spring onion/scallion, finely chopped, then soaked in cold water for 10 minutes to remove bitterness, drained
10 g/⅓ oz. fresh mint, finely chopped across the fibre
10 g/⅓ oz. peeled and thinly sliced fresh ginger
10 g/⅓ oz. fresh coriander/cilantro, finely chopped
6 red radishes, thinly sliced, then soaked in cold water to remove bitterness, drained

SERVES 4

Combine all the peanut butter sauce ingredients and blitz using a food processor or a hand-held stick blender.

If the texture is too thick to pour, then add 2 tablespoons of water.

Mix all the yakumi toppings together in a bowl. Dice the tofu into four cubes, then place on individual serving plates. Pour the peanut sauce over the tofu, then garnish each portion with the toppings and serve. The peanut butter sauce will keep in the fridge for up to 3 days.

TABERU LA-YU TOFU

300 g/10½ oz. silken tofu, drained
4 tbsp Taberu La-Yu Sauce (see page 36)
20 g/¾ oz. store-bought fried shallots

SERVES 4

Scoop a large spoonful of silken tofu into 4 individual serving bowls, then pour the taberu la-yu sauce on top. Garnish with fried shallots.

SATSUMA AGE

Satsuma age are deep-fried fish cakes, originating from Kagoshima prefecture in southern Japan. They're a popular addition to odens and udon noodles, but can also be enjoyed on their own in bentos and as side dishes. In this recipe, I give these patties a South East Asian twist by adding some coriander/cilantro to liven up the flavours, and a fish sauce-based dipping sauce for a final umami kick! I also added tofu to the prawn/shrimp mix for a softer texture.

400 g/14 oz. medium-firm tofu, well drained
180 g/6½ oz. raw king prawns/jumbo shrimp, peeled and deveined
1 tsp peeled and finely grated fresh ginger
1 tsp grated garlic
½ tsp golden caster/granulated sugar
½ tsp fine salt
1–3 tbsp katakuriko (potato starch), as needed
10 g/⅓ oz. fresh coriander/cilantro leaves
grated zest of 1 lemon
750 ml/3¼ cups vegetable oil, for frying

DIPPING SAUCE
2 tbsp fish sauce
1 tbsp rice vinegar
1 tbsp freshly squeezed lemon juice
2 tsp golden caster/granulated sugar
1 tsp toasted sesame oil
1 red chilli, deseeded and finely chopped

MAKES 20 BALLS

To remove the excess water from the tofu, wrap the block of tofu in several layers of kitchen paper and place it in a shallow tray with a rim. Set a flat, heavy pan or a plate with some books on top to compress the tofu and leave for 30 minutes.

Meanwhile, mix all the dipping sauce ingredients together in a small bowl and set aside.

Finely chop half of the prawns/shrimp or pulse in the food processor to make a paste. Roughly chop the remaining prawns/shrimp.

Unwrap the tofu and smash it into a smooth paste in a large bowl using your hands (or you can use a food processor for this too). Mix the prawn/shrimp paste and chopped prawns/shrimp with the tofu paste in the bowl. Add the ginger, garlic, sugar and salt. If the mixture is too wet or loose to be shaped into balls, mix in the katakuriko, a spoonful at a time, until the texture is firm enough to be shaped. Roughly tear the coriander/cilantro into the bowl, add the lemon zest and mix to evenly combine.

Heat the vegetable oil in a large, heavy-based saucepan to 180°C (350°F) over high heat. To check that the oil is ready, drop a little of the tofu mixture into the oil. If it gently sizzles, it's ready. Reduce the heat to medium to maintain the temperature.

Scoop out heaped tablespoons of the tofu mixture and shape each spoonful into a ball. You should get roughly 20 balls.

Depending on the size of your pan, you can fry the fish cakes in two or three batches. Gently drop the balls into the prepared oil. Deep-fry for about 4 minutes, turning them a couple of times, until they are golden. Remove from the oil with a slotted spoon and transfer to a cooling rack to drain the excess oil.

Serve the satsuma age hot with the dipping sauce (they are still tasty cold too). Mini bamboo skewers are useful for serving these at a cocktail party.

OKONOMIYAKI

I had to include an okonomiyaki recipe here, this dish being one of the most popular Japanese street foods. In my previous book, *Atsuko's Japanese Kitchen*, I gave you the traditional recipe which uses yamaimo. This ingredient helps make the pancake fluffy on the inside in contrast with the crispy outside. However, I realized that this root vegetable can be quite hard to find, so I devised this new recipe without the infamous yamaimo! The trick is to beat the finely chopped cabbage and eggs until the mixture becomes frothy. The batter will then stay light and airy as it cooks. Have a go at it and enjoy being creative with your toppings!

PANCAKE BATTER

125 g/1 cup minus 1 tbsp plain/
  all-purpose flour
1 tsp baking powder
150 ml/⅔ cup chilled Dashi of
  your choice (see pages 32–33)

FILLINGS

250 g/9 oz. green or white cabbage,
  very finely chopped
2 UK large/US extra-large eggs
2 spring onions/scallions, very finely
  chopped
2 tbsp vegetable oil

TOPPINGS (CHOOSE FROM THE FOLLOWING)

40 g/1½ oz. raw prawns/shrimp
  or raw squid cut into rings
2 mushrooms, sliced
2 tbsp sweetcorn/corn kernels
50 g/½ cup grated mature Cheddar

TO SERVE

120 ml/½ cup okonomiyaki sauce
90 ml/⅓ cup Japanese mayonnaise
10 g/⅓ oz. bonito flakes
2 tsp aonori seaweed flakes
  (optional)

20-cm/8-inch frying pan/skillet

MAKES 2 SMALL PORTIONS

To make the batter, sift the flour and baking powder into a mixing bowl. Add the dashi slowly, whisking to break up any lumps of flour (be careful not to overmix). Put the batter into the fridge to rest for 15 minutes.

Put the cabbage in a separate large bowl and add the eggs. Whisk well until the mixture becomes frothy. Fold in the spring onions/scallions. Add the batter to the cabbage in two batches, stirring gently until combined.

Heat a 20-cm/8-inch frying pan/skillet over high heat. When hot, oil the surface of the pan with 1 tbsp vegetable oil. Add half of the pancake mixture to the pan. Reduce the heat to medium, then sprinkle your chosen toppings (prawns/shrimp, squid, mushrooms and/or sweetcorn) over the pancake while the surface is still wet. Make sure you don't add too much and that the toppings are in a single layer. Sprinkle over the grated cheese last, which will melt over your other toppings.

Cook for 2 minutes, or until the bottom of the pancake turns brown and small bubbles appear around the outside. Turn over using a spatula, then cook the other side for 4–6 minutes, depending on the thickness. (Don't press down on the pancakes as they cook or they will become hard.)

When the other side is cooked and the cheese has become crisp, turn the okonomiyaki over again and cook for 1 more minute. Turn out onto a plate and repeat the process with the remaining batter and ingredients.

Place the okonomiyaki on individual serving plates and spread the okonomiyaki sauce all over with the back of a spoon. Squeeze the Japanese mayonnaise over in parallel horizontal lines at intervals of 5 mm/¼ inch, then drag a cocktail stick/toothpick across in the opposite direction at similar intervals to make a crosshatch pattern across the mayonnaise. This decoration is optional but fun to try.

Sprinkle the okonomiyaki with bonito flakes and watch them 'dance' in the heat! Add aonori seaweed flakes for extra flavour if you like.

KIMCHI NABE

Japanese love Korean food but it can be a bit spicy for us, so we tend to recreate Korean recipes, Japanese-style, with less heat in them! This recipe is a take on the famous Korean Kimchi Jjigae. It's the perfect recipe for cold, wintry days. Typically, family or friends gather around one nabe pot and cook the ingredients together on a stove. It's a truly communal dish, and real soul food. You can also serve kimchi nabe after having served a couple of starter dishes to round off the meal in a warming and comforting way.

1 tbsp vegetable oil

1 tsp finely chopped garlic

1 tsp peeled and finely chopped fresh ginger

800 ml/3⅓ cups Dashi of your choice (see pages 32–33)

1 tbsp toasted sesame oil

2 tbsp mirin

1½ tbsp gochujang

4 tbsp white miso

1 pak choi, halved lengthways

2 Chinese cabbage or Savoy cabbage leaves, diced

1 leek, sliced

100 g/3½ oz. mixed Japanese mushrooms such as shimeji, shiitake and enoki, trimmed

300 g/10½ oz. silken tofu, carefully diced into 4–6 chunks

150 g/5½ oz. kimchi

2 spring onions/scallions, thinly sliced, to serve

SERVES 4

For the soup, put the vegetable oil in a medium saucepan over medium heat. Add the garlic and ginger and fry for 1 minute to infuse some flavour into the oil.

Add the dashi to the pan and bring to the boil. Once boiling, add the toasted sesame oil, mirin, gochujang and miso. Stir until the miso has dissolved.

Add the pak choi, cabbage, leek, mushrooms, tofu and kimchi, then bring to the boil again. Turn down the heat and simmer for 5 minutes.

Turn the heat off and let the soup rest for 20 minutes to allow the flavour to develop. Reheat it gently and serve in bowls garnished with spring onions/scallions.

ATSUAGE TOFU

厚揚げ豆腐
DEEP-FRIED THICK TOFU

Atsuage is such a popular ingredient in Japanese cooking that you can find it in any supermarket/grocery store in Japan, or even at your local Asian supermarket. It is simply deep-fried tofu – no need for batter here! Making it at home is so easy and worthwhile. Eat it freshly made, as it is, with a few toppings and some sauce. It's crunchy and slightly nutty on the outside but very nutritious, being a plant-based protein. You can keep leftovers for up to 3 days and add them to soups or stir-fries.

400-g /14-oz. pack of
   medium-firm tofu, drained
750 ml/3¼ cups vegetable oil,
   plus extra if needed

TO SERVE
2 red radishes
2 spring onions/scallions
1 tbsp toasted sesame oil
Banno Sauce (see page 35)
   or soy sauce
English mustard

SERVES 4–6

To remove the excess water from the tofu, wrap the block of tofu in several layers of kitchen paper and place it in a shallow tray with a rim. Set a flat, heavy pan or a plate with some books on top to compress the tofu and leave for 30 minutes. Discard the paper.

Pour the vegetable oil into a heavy-based saucepan (20–24 cm/ 8–9 inches in diameter should be big enough for cooking the block of tofu). Make sure that the amount of oil in the pan will be deep enough to just cover the tofu with enough space for it to cook and sizzle – you may need to add a little more oil depending on the size of your pan.

Start to bring the temperature of the oil to 160°C (320°F) over medium-high heat. It doesn't matter if the tofu is added when the oil is slightly cooler, so slide the tofu gently into the oil using a large spatula. When it starts to gently sizzle with bubbles around the tofu you know the temperature of the oil is correct. Reduce the heat to medium to maintain the temperature and deep-fry for 10 minutes. The tofu should be gently sizzling the whole time it is cooking. Turn the tofu over halfway through the cooking time, using long tongs or a heatproof spatula and chopsticks.

Prepare a cooling rack close to the pan with the tofu. When the tofu gets golden brown and crispy on the surface, remove it from the oil carefully with tongs and transfer to the cooling rack.

Thinly slice the red radishes. Cut the spring onion/scallions into 4-cm/ 1½-inch lengths, then thinly slice these lengthways into small strands. Soak the radish slices and strands of spring onion/scallion in separate bowls of cold water for 10 minutes, then drain well.

Dice the block of fried tofu, then place on a serving plate. If you like, you can alternate the fried side and the white inside of the cubes of tofu to create a chequerboard effect. Garnish with the spring onion/scallion and radish on top. Drizzle over some toasted sesame oil and serve with banno sauce and English mustard. This is delicious served warm or cold.

DASHIMAKI TAMAGO SANSYU

Dashimaki is a rolled omelette, which combines eggs with dashi. Compared to its cousin, tamagoyaki, dashimaki is more moist, with a juicier texture. It's a popular dish at izakayas, often enjoyed with a glass of sake. It's also delicious with some cod's roe for a smokier taste or with sheets of nori for striking presentation. I like to use a rectangular tamagoyaki pan to make dashimaki as it's easier to roll the eggs.

DASHIMAKI & SPRING ONION/SCALLION

60 ml/¼ cup chilled Dashi of your choice (see pages 32–33)
½ tsp light soy sauce
1 tsp mirin
pinch of sea salt
4 UK large/US extra-large eggs
2 spring onions/scallions, thinly sliced
2 tbsp vegetable oil, for frying

TO SERVE
Banno Sauce (see page 35)
grated radish
finely chopped spring onion/scallion

DASHIMAKI & NORI

60 ml/¼ cup chilled Dashi of your choice (see pages 32–33)
½ tsp light soy sauce
1 tsp mirin
pinch of sea salt
4 UK large/US extra-large eggs
4 nori sheets (9 x 10 cm/3½ x 4 inches, depending on the size of the pan you use)
2 tbsp vegetable oil, for frying

TO SERVE
mayonnaise
soy sauce
shichimi spice mix

DASHIMAKI & COD'S ROE

60 ml/¼ cup chilled Dashi of your choice (see pages 32–33)
½ tsp light soy sauce
1 tsp mirin
pinch of sea salt
4 UK large/US extra-large eggs
60 g/2 oz. smoked cod's roe, membrane removed, diced
2 tbsp vegetable oil, for frying

ANKAKE SAUCE (JAPANESE GRAVY)
200 ml/generous ¾ cup Kombu & Katsuobushi Dashi (see page 33)
2 tbsp light soy sauce
2 tbsp mirin
1 tbsp katakuriko (potato starch) mixed with 1½ tbsp cold water in a cup

cooking chopsticks
square or rectangular omelette pan/ skillet, approx. 15 x 18 cm/6 x 7 inches

SERVES 4

Mix the dashi, light soy sauce, mirin and salt together in a cup until the salt has dissolved. Set aside.

Break the eggs into a large bowl. Use chopsticks to break the egg yolks and mix them together thoroughly with the egg whites so no lumps of white remain. Pour the dashi mixture into the eggs and stir gently. If you are making the spring onion/scallion variation, add the spring onions/scallions to the egg mixture and mix well.

Place the omelette pan/skillet over high heat. Put the vegetable oil into a small bowl and soak a piece of kitchen paper in the oil. Use chopsticks to carefully spread the oil-soaked paper around the pan to lightly grease it. Make sure the pan is hot, then pour one-fifth of the egg mixture into the pan, tilting it to evenly spread the mixture. Use your chopsticks to gently burst the bubbles that appear on the egg as it cooks.

When the omelette is half-cooked (within about 10 seconds), take the pan off the heat briefly.

If you are making the nori variation, place a sheet of nori on top of the egg. For the smoked cod's roe variation, place all of the smoked cod's roe on the egg near the back

Recipe continued overleaf >>

of the pan. For all three variations, roll the omelette up towards you using the chopsticks, then push the roll to the back of the pan.

Spread over another layer of oil in the pan using the oil-soaked kitchen paper. Pour in another fifth of the remaining egg mixture, tilting the pan so that the new mixture spreads out and under the first egg roll. Within 10 seconds, when the mixture is half-cooked, add another sheet of nori if you are making the nori variation, then roll the first egg roll towards you so that the new omelette wraps around it to make one larger roll.

Repeat this process three more times to use up the remaining egg mixture (and nori for the nori variation). Each time, try to spread the egg under the main roll as quickly as possible so that they stick together.

After the last roll, turn the heat off. Put clean kitchen paper or a bamboo mat on a plate and tightly wrap the egg roll in it. Leave for 3 minutes. Unwrap the egg roll and cut into 2-cm/¾-inch thick slices.

To make the ankake sauce for the Dashimaki & Cod's Roe variation, bring the dashi, soy sauce and mirin to the boil in a saucepan.

Reduce the heat to low, stir the katakuriko and water mixture well, then slowly whisk it into the dashi. Bring to the boil again to thicken the sauce, then remove from the heat.

Serve your dashimaki tamago warm with the suggested dipping sauce for the recipe you have chosen.

KARE
ARANCINI

My husband being Italian, we enjoy the food of Italy in our house, so this recipe is a little wink his way. It came into existence one day when I had some leftover rice and Japanese curry, and thought, why not make use of it in Japanese-inspired arancini?! They turned out delicious and got the approval of the Italian of the house. A simple way to make Japanese curry is to use curry roux, which you can find easily in large supermarkets or Asian grocery stores these days.

250 g/9 oz. cooked Japanese rice
  (see pages 30–31)
12 quail eggs, boiled for 5 minutes,
  cooled then peeled
50 g/generous ⅓ cup plain/
  all-purpose flour
1 UK large/US extra-large egg,
  lightly beaten
100 g/2⅓ cups panko breadcrumbs
750 ml/3¼ cups vegetable oil,
  for frying

JAPANESE CURRY
1 tbsp vegetable oil
60 g/2 oz. onion, finely chopped
50 g/1¾ oz. Japanese curry roux,
  chopped

TO SERVE
sweet smoked paprika
mayonnaise

MAKES 12

To make the Japanese curry, heat a medium saucepan over high heat. Add the vegetable oil, then the onion. Turn the heat down very low and fry the onion for about 10 minutes until softened.

Add 300 ml/1¼ cups water to the pan and bring to the boil. Turn the heat down and simmer the onions for 5 minutes, then turn the heat off. Once slightly cooled, add the curry roux, then stir until dissolved.

Bring the curry back to the boil, then simmer over low heat while stirring for 1–2 minutes until thickened. Add the cooked rice, stir and simmer for 5 minutes. Turn the heat off and leave the curry rice until cool enough to handle. The consistency will still be quite loose, but the texture will become thicker as it cools.

Dip your hands into water to stop the rice from sticking when you handle it. Divide the curry rice into 12 balls, roughly the size and shape of ping pong balls. Flatten a rice ball in your hand and put a boiled quail egg in the middle. Wrap the rice around the egg and roll it into a round shape. Repeat with the remaining rice balls and eggs.

Put the flour, egg and panko breadcrumbs in three separate bowls. Coat each rice ball in the flour, then the egg and finally the breadcrumbs. Set aside for 15 minutes at room temperature to allow the coating to set.

Heat the vegetable oil in a medium, heavy-based saucepan to 180°C (350°F) over high heat. To check that the oil is ready, drop a few panko breadcrumbs into the oil. If they float to the surface and gently sizzle, the oil is ready. Reduce the heat to medium to maintain the temperature.

Gently lower half the balls into the oil and deep-fry for about 3 minutes until golden brown, turning them over a couple of times as they fry. Remove from the oil with a slotted spoon and transfer to a cooling rack. Repeat the cooking process for the remaining rice balls.

Cut the rice balls in half if you are serving them at a cocktail party. Sprinkle with sweet smoked paprika and serve with mayo.

INDEX

Senior Designer Megan Smith
Editor Alice Sambrook
Contributing Editor Elsa Gleeson
Art Director Leslie Harrington
Editorial Director Julia Charles
Head of Production
    Patricia Harrington
Publisher Cindy Richards

Food Stylist Atsuko Ikeda
Prop Stylist Hannah Wilkinson
Indexer Hilary Bird
Illustrator Claire Harrup

Published in 2022 by
Ryland Peters & Small
20–21 Jockey's Fields
London WC1R 4BW
and
341 East 116th Street
New York, NY 10029

www.rylandpeters.com

10 9 8 7 6 5 4 3 2

Text © Atsuko Ikeda 2022

Design, illustration and
commissioned photography ©
Ryland Peters & Small 2022

ISBN 978-1-78879-430-5

A CIP record for this book
is available from the Britsih
Library.

US Library of Congress CIP
data has been applied for.

Printed in China

NOTES
• Both British (Metric) and
American (Imperial plus US
cups) measurements are
included in these recipes for
your convenience. However it
is important to work with one
set of measurements and not
alternate between the two
within a recipe.
• All spoon measurements are
level unless otherwise specified.
• Uncooked or partially cooked
eggs should not be served
to the very old, frail, young
children, pregnant women
or those with compromised
immune systems.
• When following a recipe
which uses raw fish or meat,
always ensure you buy sashimi-
quality ingredients and use on
the day of purchase. Raw fish
or meat should not be served
to the very old, frail, young
children, pregnant women
or those with compromised
immune systems, without
medical advice.
• When a recipe calls for the
grated zest of citrus fruit, buy
unwaxed fruit and wash well
before using. If you can only
find treated fruit, scrub well in
warm soapy water before using.

FOOD SAFETY NOTICE
The information contained
within this book is intended
as a general guide based on
the author's recipe development
and experience. Although all
reasonable care has been
taken in the preparation of this
book, neither the publishers
nor the author can accept any
liability for any consequence
from the use thereof, or the
information contained therein.
Please consult an up-to-date
government source on food
safety for further information.

ACKNOWLEDGEMENTS

This is my third book working with my wonderful team. After producing *Sushi Made Simple* and *Atsuko's Japanese Kitchen*, which I am so proud of, we're back! Stronger and more inspired than ever!

My endless gratitude to the people who helped me bring this book to fruition starts with my publisher, Cindy Richards, you've been one of the most influential people in my life. Thank you for believing in me and letting me grow as a cookbook author.

I am always thankful to my editorial and design team: Julia Charles, Leslie Harrington, and Megan Smith, thank you for your patience and your commitment to understanding my work. All of your hard work towards this book is immeasurable.

Alice Sambrook is a key person in my book publishing journey. I am so grateful that you are back again working on this book too! I really appreciate your attention to detail and making this book relevant to a wide audience. No one apart from you, could have done this job to the same high quality with which you delivered it.

I can't thank my dear friend Elsa Gleeson enough. She has the art of encouraging, correcting and directing me on every occasion. She is also the only one who bought dozens of copies of my cookbooks to give as presents to her family and friends. Your contribution writing introductions has been a true influence on this book.

My favourite photographer, Yuki Sugiura. It has been a real pleasure to work with you, Yuki-chan. You're not only an incredibly talented photographer, but you also inspire me in so many ways as a person.

Claire Harrup, I am so lucky to have found you! Your illustrations add a modern yet personal touch to this book making it fresh and relevant.

Hannah Wilkinson, you have such a great eye for selecting all these amazing eclectic props which match the theme of this book perfectly. My long term assistant Michiyo Sakaida for inspiring me and providing me with your precious support while doing the food styling on the photoshoots.

Very special thanks to John Moore, Atsuko's Kitchen's landlord, in East London. Your generosity of letting us use your beautiful ceramics and props for our photoshoots made the food look stunning and more attractive than they could ever have been.

Aya Nakagawa at Colenimo for providing me with beautiful furoshiki cloths for the photoshoot. It added a visual sense of Japanese culture to the book.

To my friends and assistants, for their contributions and advice throughout the development of this book: Anita Lim, Ivana Sestak, Eime Tobari, Emma Spinelli, Emma Betts, Noriko Tanaka, Mari Takahashi, Masako Sato, Hiroe Hamilton, and Yoko Kawabata. All of you have given me the confidence to create the recipes in this book.

I will never thank my parents enough, Yuriko and Hideki Ikeda in Japan. I missed you so much while making this book (I haven't been able to go back to Japan at this point in almost 3.5 years!). I cannot wait to have otsumami with you when I can finally go back! Ornella and Marco Rossi, my Italian parents, you inspired me to infuse some of these recipes with some Italian flavours, and my husband, Michele Rossi, and our boys Nicolo and Enzo. It would not have been possible to progress on my publishing journey without your continuous support. Finally, we can now enjoy some well-deserved quality time together with plenty of otsumami to indulge in!